CHICAGO BLUES SLIDE GUITAR

THE COMPLETE *and* DEFINITIVE GUIDE

To access video visit:
www.halleonard.com/mylibrary

Enter Code
7505-6794-8407-0331

Cover photo courtesy of Bob Margolin

ISBN 978-1-4950-5893-6

Visit Hal Leonard Online at
www.halleonard.com

Contact us:
Hal Leonard
7777 West Bluemound Road
Milwaukee, WI 53213
Email: info@halleonard.com

In Europe, contact:
Hal Leonard Europe Limited
42 Wigmore Street
Marylebone, London, W1U 2RN
Email: info@halleonardeurope.com

In Australia, contact:
Hal Leonard Australia Pty. Ltd.
4 Lentara Court
Cheltenham, Victoria, 3192 Australia
Email: info@halleonard.com.au

CONTENTS

About the Video

To access the accompanying videos for download or streaming, simply visit **www.halleonard.com/mylibrary** and enter the code from page 1 of this book.

DEDICATION AND ACKNOWLEDGMENTS

I dedicate my part of this book to my partner in blues guitar, Dave Rubin. This is our third collaboration founded on friendship, respect, and love of the music. Thanks to the Hal Leonard team and especially Jeff Schroedl for putting us together. I try to honor Muddy Waters, the man and his music, in everything I play, especially slide guitar. And thank you for your interest.

Bob Margolin
North Carolina 2020

I dedicate this book to the late John Campbell, an unsung blues guitar hero who left us too soon. Thanks to Jeff Schroedl, Kurt Plahna, and everyone else at Hal Leonard for their unconditional support over the years. And, of course, to my "Blues Brother," Steady Rollin' Bob Margolin.

Dave Rubin
NYC 2020

PREFACE

Those who own *Chicago Blues Rhythm Guitar* (Hal Leonard) will already know the exceptional teaching skills of Steady Rollin' Bob Margolin. They are derived from his unwavering dedication to the blues, great talent as a player *and* writer, decades on bandstands, and his unsurpassed experience with Muddy Waters, among other blues legends. It is again my pleasure to be his co-author on a topic near and dear to both of our hearts. Join us as we traverse the long and winding blues highway of Chicago blues slide guitar from its beginnings in the 1930s up to the present day.

Dave Rubin

It Sings!

Your guitar plays more than sensual rhythms and grooves. When you play electric slide guitar, you bring more vibrato, flexible pitch, and the same kind of chops that make a singer exciting. That is exactly why this technique thrills blues guitarists and audiences more than any other I have seen in over 50 years on blues bandstands. Whether you play it with heartbreaking subtle nuance or kick-ass flash, or sometimes combining both, your slide guitar playing is the essence of moving blues music.

Without a slide, a similar effect is achieved by bending strings, sliding between notes, and using finger vibrato to make the note cry. But the creators of that style sometimes explicitly revealed they learned to play that way because slide did not come naturally to them. B.B. King humbly explained that, unlike his country blues slide guitar master cousin Bukka White, he had "stupid fingers" and couldn't slide, so he developed his famous finger vibrato. There are plenty of players who are great at both in a wide palette of deep blues guitar expression.

In the late 1970s, Johnny Winter was producing albums for Muddy Waters. I played on the recordings and tried to be helpful to both. They are on the short list of the greatest slide guitarists. It was an opportunity to learn from Johnny as well as Muddy. I remember a conversation with Johnny where we seemed to realize at the same time that a singing guitarist's vocal and guitar vibrato were usually identical in speed. Electric Chicago blues slide guitar is your personal, signature voice, and we humbly hope to inspire you with this book. You can browse it and look for a subject or video that interests you. You don't have to view it in sequence for any part of it to make sense. Please join Dave Rubin and me as we explore the history, technique, and musical beauty of electric Chicago blues slide guitar.

Bob Margolin

Fig 1: This is Chicago blues slide guitar.

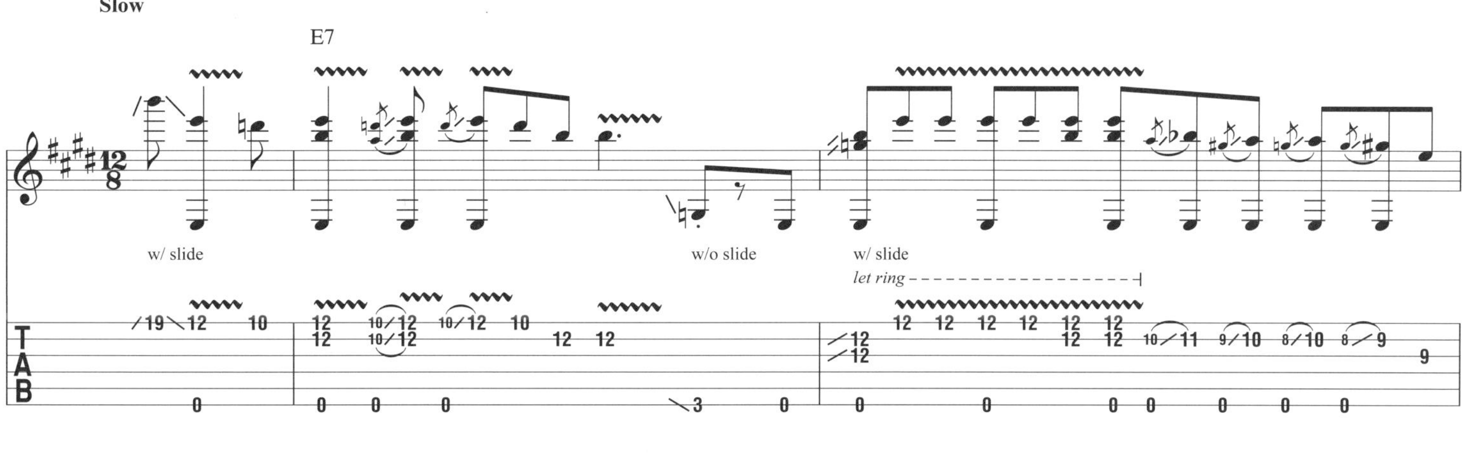

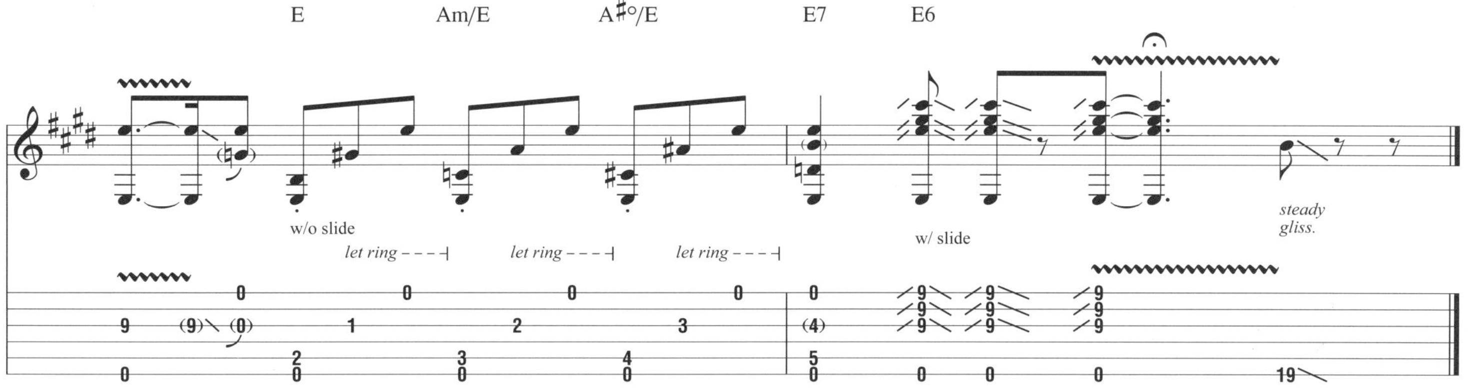

GLASS, BRASS, AND STEEL: A BRIEF HISTORY OF SLIDE GUITAR

by Dave Rubin

Blues guitarists have been sliding glass, brass, and steel along with sticks, stones, and bones on steel strings for over 100 years to create the infinite microtones and crying vibrato that encompass the full palette of emotions—from dark-hued despair to brilliant heights of ecstasy. When the steroidal boost of electricity is injected, a sound as thick as Mississippi mud with near endless sustain is the result.

Out of Africa? The Birth of Recorded Blues Slide Guitar

The blues is a musical language in which the slide or bottleneck guitar is one of the primary texts. It is also the first blues guitar technique mentioned by W.C. Handy (1873–1958) and the first style of blues to be recorded solo by an African-American guitarist. In an oft-told tale, the self-anointed "Father of the Blues" was waiting for a train at the station in Tutwiler, Mississippi, in 1903, and heard an itinerant blues guitarist sliding with a pocket knife. The experience for Handy literally transformed the classically-trained composer and led to his embrace of the cultural (not to mention commercial) value of the blues.

When bottleneck pioneer Sylvester Weaver (1897–1960) went to New York City and waxed the groundbreaking solo instrumentals "Guitar Blues" and "Guitar Rag" in November of 1923, he set the (slide) bar high for future blues guitarists. Both tracks boast exceptionally clean intonation along with the expressive blending of single notes and chords that would become the hallmark for blues guitarists during the Delta and country blues eras and into the future.

Handy initially described the music played in Tutwiler "as in the manner of Hawaiian guitarists" and therein lies one of the controversies surrounding the development of the blues. The sliding of natural objects along a taut string or "diddley bow" was an element of African culture that was likely retained when the slaves came to America, only to reappear in Mississippi when the blues germinated some time after the Civil War. Around the same time, Hawaiian "slack key" guitar with a slider was being played in the islands. By 1912, bands of Hawaiian musicians were touring the mainland and a craze for their music *and* the blues began concurrently. Lil' Ed Williams (1955–) explains, "It might have come from Africa or Hawaii. But, all the old time slide musicians, the first music they played was gospel. Even the slaves were singing gospel before they started singing about how the master was 'doing them.'"

The First String Team

Whatever the truth, both genres relied on open tunings. Solo country blues guitarists used the harmonious open strings inherent in open G, D, A, and E tunings to build steady grooves upon which to overlay steely riffs and licks. Blind Willie Johnson (1902–1947), one of the most phenomenal of gospel and blues bottleneckers, refined his art to where he stunningly mimicked his vocal melody on monumental classics like "It's Nobody's Fault but Mine" and his chilling narrative about the sinking of the Titanic, "God Moves on the Water." His seemingly free form instrumental "Dark Was the Night – Cold Was the Ground" is justly lauded as a masterpiece of American vernacular music. Charley Patton (1891–1934), the "Father of the Delta Blues," built his best-known slide numbers like "Pony Blues" and "High Water Everywhere" on relentless rhythmic drive, rather than intricate licks, combined with a booming, declamatory vocal delivery that was perfect for the funky, raucous juke joints in which he held sway.

During the remaining decade of the Delta blues era, the bottleneck came to represent the deepest, darkest, heaviest blues as giants of the genre continued to stride across the land. Eddie "Son" House (1890?–1988) exhibited a brutal rhythmic attack, forging a rock solid template with "My Black Mama," "Preachin' the Blues," and "Walking Blues" for some of the most important blues artists who would follow. John Mooney (1955–), who spent time jamming with House in the 1960s, says the guitar legend "Could play variations on 'Walking Blues' for 45 minutes at a time." Son's most famous musical progeny was Robert Johnson (1911–1938), who based his version of "Walkin' Blues" on "My Black Mama" and recast "Preachin' Blues" into a virtuosic bottlenecking extravaganza. His "Terraplane Blues," "Cross Road Blues," "Come On in My Kitchen," "If I Had Possession Over Judgment Day," and "Traveling Riverside Blues" set the benchmark for masterful execution, intonation, and the superior integration of singing single-note lines and chordal forms.

The End of Rambling

When Robert Johnson was killed in 1938, it essentially signaled the end of acoustic country blues as electric combo blues was about to change the global template following the introduction of Gibson's innovative electric ES-150 guitar in 1936. Left to hit the highway were many other brilliant bottleneck men, including Blind Willie McTell (1901–1959) from Georgia, a 12-string guitarist of exceptional skill. Likewise, left-handed James "Kokomo" Arnold, known as one of the fastest bottleneckers around, had influenced Robert Johnson's immortal "Sweet Home Chicago" with his "Old Original Kokomo Blues." Booker T. "Bukka" Washington White (1904–1977) saw his career "slide" upward when he went to Chicago at Big Bill Broonzy's behest in 1937. He was one of the last raw country bluesmen to still be plying his trade by 1940 while often playing lap steel-style like Arnold.

Coming to Chicago from Mississippi, Muddy Waters (1913–1983) popularized amplified electric slide first in open G tuning and then in standard tuning starting in 1949. He also sang with great blues power as he broke through, and so did...

Elmo: Carving the Rosetta Stone for Electric Slide

When Elmore James whipped his slider over the classic triplet riff on his monumental, over-amped version of Robert Johnson's "Dust My Broom" in Mississippi in 1951, he stormed the traditional country blues barricades. He went beyond what was happening in Chicago, with a clanging clarion call featuring slide over thumping boogie bass patterns in a thrilling combination, which is quintessential electric Chicago blues. Almost overnight, according to former Muddy Waters drummer Willie "Big Eyes" Smith, harp blowers were feeling the heat from slide guitarists. His classic recordings remain the foundation of electric slide up to the current day.

Electric Chicago Blues

Towards the mid-1950s, Elmore James was joined on the scene by fellow sliders Johnny Shines, J.B. Hutto, and Honeyboy Edwards, among others. Shines moved to Chi-Town in 1941 and made his electric bones with a masterful series of recordings in 1952. J.B. Hutto arrived in the Windy City with his family in 1949 and would make a name for himself in the 1960s with his scalding post-Elmore style.

David "Honeyboy" Edwards is possibly the lone exception among former Delta blues guitarists: He played almost exclusively in standard tuning. He felt that, to paraphrase, "Real blues guitarists don't use open tunings." Bob Margolin responds, "With great respect for Honeyboy, does that mean that Son House wasn't a 'real' blues guitarist? What about minor chords? I have used open G minor and open D minor tunings on original songs. The minor tunings sound eerie, enhancing dark lyrics. Is it blues when I do that? Call it what you want." Also relocating from the Delta in the early 1950s was Chester Arthur "Howlin' Wolf" Burnett, the legendary singer and occasional slide guitar player.

By the 1960s and the Blues Revival, Earl Hooker (1930–1970) and Mississippi Fred McDowell (1904–1972) were two of the few pioneering electric slide men still at work. Hooker, along with Robert Nighthawk, was unexcelled at playing in standard tuning. McDowell had played in the Delta in the 1920s but did not make his first commercial recordings until 1965. An unreconstructed Delta bottlenecker who would play solo electric, his "You Got to Move" was covered by the Rolling Stones on *Sticky Fingers*, an ironic situation considering that he had previously recorded "I Do Not Play No Rock 'n' Roll" (1969).

Duane and Johnny

As interest in traditional blues styles and techniques began to wane in the late 1960s, a new wave of rock-influenced slide guitarists emerged. Though not from Chicago but clearly profoundly influenced by practitioners associated with the Windy City on the shores of Lake Michigan, Duane Allman (1946–1971) and Johnny Winter (1944–2014) almost single-handedly brought the art of the slide to the popular music audience, playing with a slashing sound and ferocity only matched by their authentic blues roots. Allman smolders with the Allman Brothers on "Dreams" and burns on "Statesboro Blues." Winter had an ongoing love affair with the slide, flashing his prowess innumerable times, including on his original "Mean Town Blues" and his epic version of Dylan's "Highway 61 Revisited."

Hound Dog Taylor and the New Generation

Meanwhile, flying under the radar was the inimitable Theodore Roosevelt "Hound Dog" Taylor in Chicago. He had recorded a few sides in the 1960s but did not make his album debut until 1971, as the first release for Alligator Records. His unabashedly "primitive" post-Elmore James electric blues were distilled down to almost pure emotion.

Lest one think that this "ancient" art has been relegated to the dustbin of blues history, just take a listen to some of the reigning contemporary Chicago slide kings—Bob Margolin, Lil' Ed Williams, Bernard Allison, Studebaker John, Billy Flynn, and others.

CHAPTER I:
Playing Chicago Blues Slide Guitar

by Bob Margolin

Let's start with the basics of technique and tunings. Curious beginner or experienced pro, you may discover something that enhances your playing, or you may recall the process of your own progress.

Which Finger Wears the Slide?

Unlike the bar used on a lap steel guitar, right-handed Chicago blues slide guitarists put a slide on one of the fingers of their left hand. This allows the other left-hand fingers to fret notes or make chords conventionally. Most guitarists put the slide on the pinky, ring, or middle finger. There's no right or wrong choice. If you have never played slide before, experiment with the slide on different fingers and find which feels right. The size of the finger you use will help you choose a slide.

Choosing a Slide

It's critical that your slide fits the finger you choose—not so loose that it falls off while you play, and not so tight that it hurts or that you can't get your finger in. Go for comfort, with no bad fit distracting you. Many types are available, home-made and store-bought. Steel and brass produce a harder sound. Glass and ceramic have a smoother sound.

The most common shape of a slide is a tube, but my first slide was a glass Coricidin cold medicine bottle. I like all kinds of slides, but in the real world of performing, a steel slide will not shatter if it falls on a hard floor. And if a glass slide shatters in your guitar case or pocket, the shards could slice your hand open when you reach for the slide. As I write this, I did a gig recently with a well-known great guitarist who uses glass. My metal slide sounds good in its steely way and it lasts until I lose it. Muddy Waters had a slide that a friend made for him from cutting and smoothing the edges of a metal pipe. It fit on the tip of his pinky and could only cover three strings. Your choice of material and size will depend on which finger you want to use for slide and the sound you want.

Blues Archaeology **Duane Allman famously "discovered" slide guitar while recuperating in bed from a cold and trying a Coricidin bottle on the strings.**

Acoustic Slide

The theme of this book/video is primarily *electric* Chicago blues slide guitar. That does not mean you cannot play Chicago blues on an acoustic, especially one with a pickup. There's a famous photo of the iconic Elmore James, relatively late in his career, playing a Harmony Sovereign acoustic guitar with a DeArmond clip-on pickup. I have tried recording an acoustic guitar through an amp, and it seems like I got the best of both worlds as long as I used a tiny amp for recording or didn't turn up a big amp live onstage loud enough to feed back. Acoustic guitars with pickups are more inclined to feed back than solid body or semi-hollow body guitars.

But solo or in a group, slide on an acoustic guitar sounds beautiful. There is a Chess Records album from 1964 called *Muddy Waters Folk Singer*. Maybe the title was a transparent attempt to market the album as folk music, which was very popular in the early 1960s. But what a great idea to record Muddy with acoustic instruments! Muddy played acoustic slide guitar with a very young Buddy Guy playing acoustic non-slide lead guitar. Willie Dixon played unamplified upright bass and Clifton James, Willie's drummer who was on many classic Bo Diddley songs in the 1950s, drummed softly with brushes. The album is considered not only classic but an audiophile pinnacle of sound quality. Close-miking allows you to hear sensual details of slide on strings and the subtle nuances of Muddy's voice and the instruments, especially on Muddy's solo song. It was Muddy playing blues in Chicago (ain't that Chicago blues?). The steel strings moan and snap. The album showcases the sound of acoustic Chicago blues, and Muddy's acoustic slide guitar is ultimate.

In the 1970s, when I was in Muddy's band and familiar with this album, I asked him how he felt about acoustic versus electric guitars. Muddy said he could get more out of an acoustic guitar. He also observed, "Electric guitar is an unfriendly sound!" Unsaid was that on a bandstand, with a large band, in a club or a concert, electric guitar was more practical and still extremely expressive, but with a different tonality.

Choosing a Guitar and Amp for Electric Slide

Slide guitar evokes blues music, from the elegant majesty of Mick Taylor to the funky, ragged clank of Hound Dog Taylor. Some of the best Chicago blues slide music was made on cheap equipment. There's no amp rig that is wrong unless it does not impart the sound you intend or surprise you in a good way. Try cheap equipment if you want to sound "raw." Or use the same rig you like for non-slide blues. Do you enhance your sound or switch sounds quickly with pedals? Why not? Slap echo or reverb work well with slide guitar. The classic Chicago blues players didn't use pedals as they weren't invented yet, but you can. I used an Electro-Harmonix Memory Man pedal for a subtle touch of slap echo in 1976 on Muddy's *Hard Again* album.

Setting Up a Guitar for Slide

If you prefer light strings to bend notes easily, such as a high E string of .009 or lighter, you will probably want to set up a separate guitar for your slide playing. You can slide on .010s if your slide touch is very light. If you try to slide on a guitar with light strings plus low action, the slide will clack against the frets and prevent your slide notes from ringing clearly.

A guitar deliberately set up for only slide playing should probably have at least medium-gauge strings (Muddy used .012–.056 with a .022 plain G string), similar in gauge to acoustic guitar strings; the action will be relatively high compared to easy-bending electrics. The heavy strings have a full tone and maintain tuning well, and the high action keeps the slide from hitting frets or the fingerboard itself. There is a sweet spot of string gauge and string height that enables string bending or finger trills, but allows smooth sliding too. That works for me, and I want one guitar to do it all. I've learned how to bend heavier strings as much as I want.

Blues Archaeology The ubiquitous brand of guitar strings in the prewar and early postwar era of blues guitar was Black Diamond. Though the gauges were not printed on the box, at least not until much later, by all accounts they were heavy, to say the least. In retrospect, it may have been fortuitous as the robust tone, especially on slide recordings, is still a thrill to hear.

Picking Hand Touch: Pick, Picks, or Skin?

This is the same as when you play conventional rather than slide guitar. If you have been playing for a while, you may have already chosen flat pick, thumb pick, thumb and finger picks, or no picks. You can continue this choice with your slide guitar playing and be able to pick with the precision, power, comfort, and nuance you have already developed.

Please consider this hip tip if you are not committed to a pick choice: Try not using one. You will probably develop blisters, then calluses, on the thumb and the fingers you use to pick. The process is similar to forming calluses on your fretting fingers when you first start to play. It will take a short time for them to stop hurting, but if you commit to no picks, you will find the ultimate expression of guitar, slide or non-slide. In addition, you will never need to worry about buying or losing picks again and you will always be ready to play.

About six months after I joined Muddy's band, I noticed that Hubert Sumlin with Howlin' Wolf did not use picks. He told a now well-known story of how Wolf advised him to lose the picks to play softer but more expressively. Hubert worked on it, got it great, and made it part of his trademark sound. For slide guitar with no picks, see videos of ultimate Delta blues slide guitarist Son House's picking hand technique. It's skin on strings and can work well for all blues guitarists. He popped and pulled and frailed the strings with his bare picking hand, and his playing is as powerful as it gets.

I stopped using a flat pick and went to a thumb pick right after I joined Muddy's band in 1973. A few months later, I decided to play with no picks, just toughing out the initial blisters. But I got excited the first night I tried and ripped half the thumbnail off my picking hand... blood on the strings. I had to go back to the thumb pick to finish the gig, and I have stayed with just thumb pick and bare fingers ever since. I can hold the thumb pick like a flat pick and play fast with definition. I can snap percussive notes or frail with my fingers. It works for me, but I still encourage you to find what's comfortable for you by considering everything.

Blues Archaeology When asked why he did not use a pick when playing slide, Duane Allman replied that if he did, he would have no "flesh to strings" touch.

Slide Hand Touch

Your slide notes should be crafted to the length of the notes you want to "sing," from staccato to sustained. You need to mute your notes to shape their length when you play slide guitar, just as you would without a slide. Most experienced players don't think about this process, just as a singer does not think about the physiology of vocal cords. You'll just feel the emotion your playing conveys. Let's examine the technique.

You can mute strings either with the fingers behind your slide, or with part of your picking hand—either the finger or thumb you pick with, or the heel of your hand on the bridge. Expressive slide players use different techniques or a combination in the moment.

I was advised by Muddy Waters—as he taught me to play "Can't Be Satisfied" by singing it at me rather than showing me on a guitar—to mute with the heel of my hand clamping down rhythmically on the bridge. It made my notes, high and low, sound snappy when literally clamped down percussively to stop them. It's a technique that creates emotion and drama on slide guitar. Then, when you let notes ring, they feel redeeming.

Dave Rubin and I could do an entire instruction book and video on just Muddy's guitar playing. Oh yeah, we did in 1995 for Hal Leonard with *Muddy Waters – Deep Blues* and *Muddy Waters Guitar Signature Licks*.

Sliding into a Note

When you slide to a note, you can change the feeling simply by whether you slide up to the note or down to it. To me, sliding up imparts the emotion of rising to the note, even in microseconds, and resolution when you get there is very assertive. Sliding down to a note conveys blues as well, as in landing like a fall from a higher place. Most guitarists slide up to a note and many don't play slide any other way. But a famous example of a great slide guitarist who often slides *down* to a note would be Duane Allman. His slide playing style is emotional and influential, and Derek Trucks carries it forward.

A virtuoso slide guitarist himself, Ry Cooder once described Muddy Waters' slide playing as "microtonal." Well put. Muddy did sometimes slide along one string while picking quickly—a continuous rising or falling staccato howl—to powerful effect.

Still, the most obvious way to use slide guitar is to hit one or more notes right on them, sliding neither up nor down, but conveying unadorned truth with your confident intonation and emotional vibrato.

Vibrato

Vibrato imparts emotion that moves you and your audience. It's a slide guitar producing the sensual human and canine moan, howl, or scream. More than any other single technique or nuance, vibrato is what makes slide guitar sing!

Robert Nighthawk played sophisticated non-slide guitar, but was magical when he played electric slide through a small tube amp turned up to distort naturally. His vibrato was relatively wide, compared to most other players, to great emotional effect. His vocal vibrato was similarly wide.

Muddy Waters was not bound to a single signature technique for vibrato. In the moment, he used a range of wide vibrato like Nighthawk, or could deliver a fast, stinging buzz. This "force of nature" slide guitar player always earned amazed applause and screaming after his slide solos.

Tunings

Beginning in Chapter II, we will describe and demonstrate the essence of the styles of great Chicago blues slide guitarists. We hope this discussion of techniques makes you want to play. Let's start with some conventional and a few rare tunings. Choosing the tuning is your first step to playing.

Standard Tuning

Historically, slide guitar started with players using open tunings. It is easy to sound good quickly with open tunings, but many guitar players choose both open and standard tunings. Slide in standard tuning can be easy if you have experience playing in standard because you know where the notes are.

Single-string melodies are easy to play with a slide as you can play two, three, or four notes at a time in line. Sometimes you have to move the slide more frets than your fingers could reach to find the right notes. You just have to move your slide hand up and down the neck faster. Do not think about putting your hand in one position on the neck and hitting scales. Go to the notes you're familiar with from experience. You can slide to notes, and even make new notes by sliding in between frets without picking for a vocal-like nuance.

Fig. 2: Slide in standard tuning. Find the notes "outside the box" and don't rely on scales and patterns. Take advantage of being able to find the note you want in many places on the neck in the context of your phrase.

Slow, freely

N.C.(E)

w/ slide

steady gliss.

Open Tunings

Open tunings are the traditional format for slide guitar playing. The sound or tonality alone can impart "blues." Slide masters from traditional to modern—to a few that are so advanced and original that you would call their playing a signature style—use them. We will discuss traditional open tunings and some interesting variations.

Open E

Though he played in open D, open E is the same tuning one step higher for classic Elmore James, an icon of electric Chicago blues slide. It's also used in more modern contexts in the signature styles of Duane Allman and Derek Trucks. Johnny Winter really supercharged his open E slide playing blues with a rock 'n' roll spirit. The tuning is, low to high, E-B-E-G#-B-E—by only changing three strings from standard tuning. If you want to play along with Elmore James songs, you'll want to tune your guitar to open D, one step lower than open E.

Blues Archaeology **Blues guitar hero Sylvester Weaver recorded the instrumentals "Guitar Blues" and "Guitar Rag" in open E. The latter highly influential tune was rerecorded by Weaver in 1927 and subsequently covered by Harvey and Johnson (1930), Bob Wills as "Steel Guitar Rag" (questionably attributed to his steel guitarist Leon McAuliffe in 1936), and Earl Hooker (1951).**

Fig. 3: Chicago blues slide licks in E in the classic style. Also, you'll see some of the most common non-slide licks, like the barre lick on the IV chord which becomes easier in open E than in standard tuning. And the walk-down on the turnaround can be done with one finger. Combining slide and fingered licks within a verse increases the drama of each. 1+1=3.

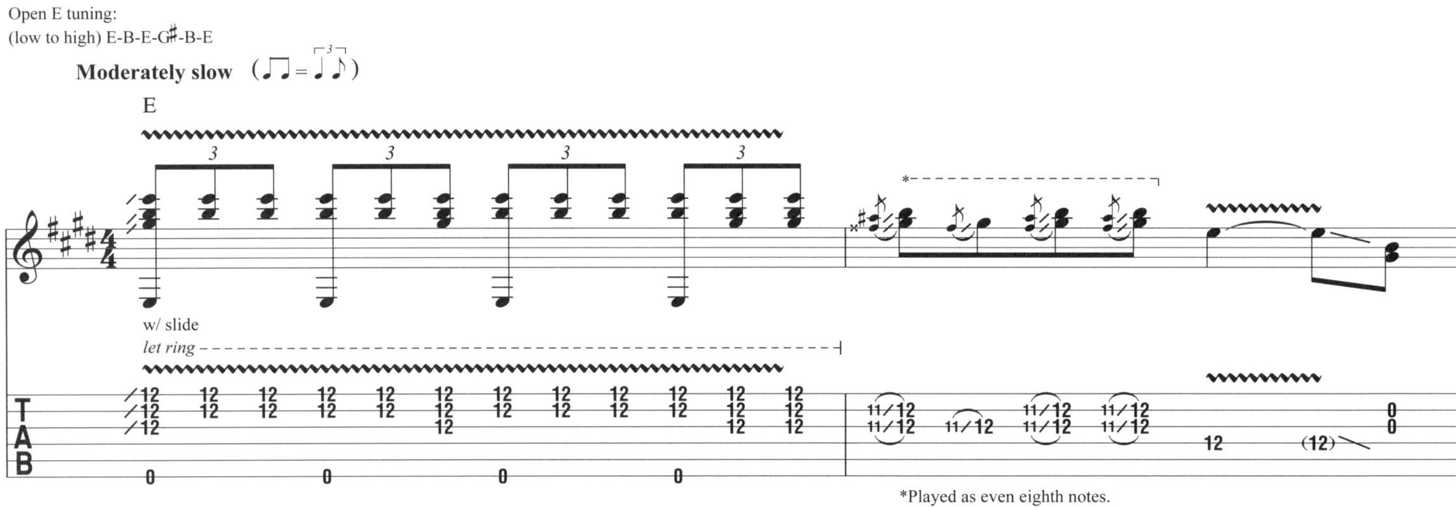

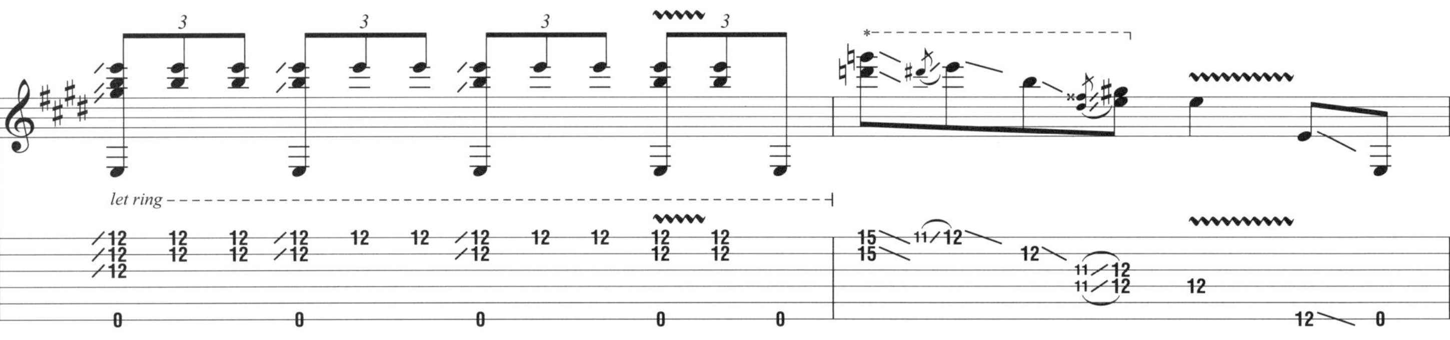

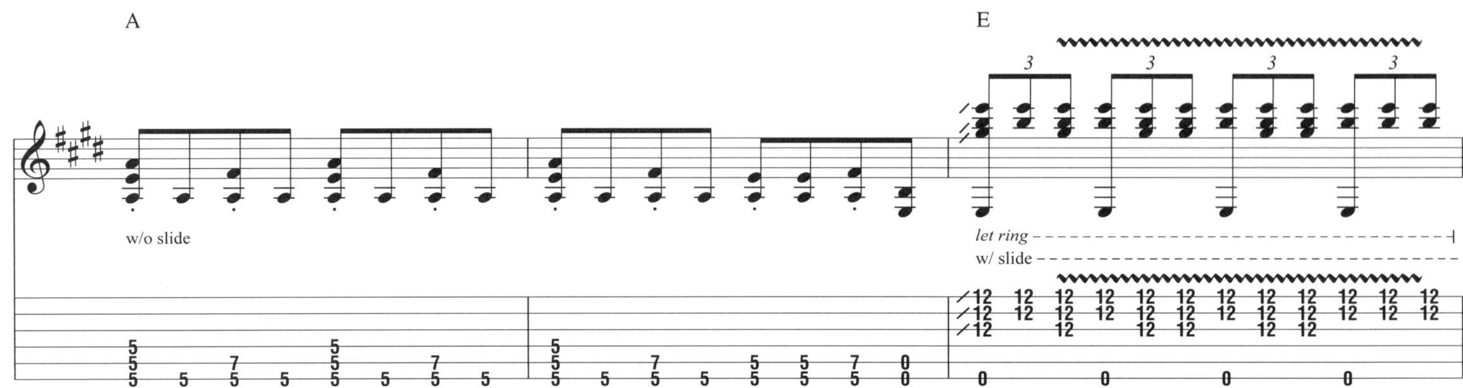

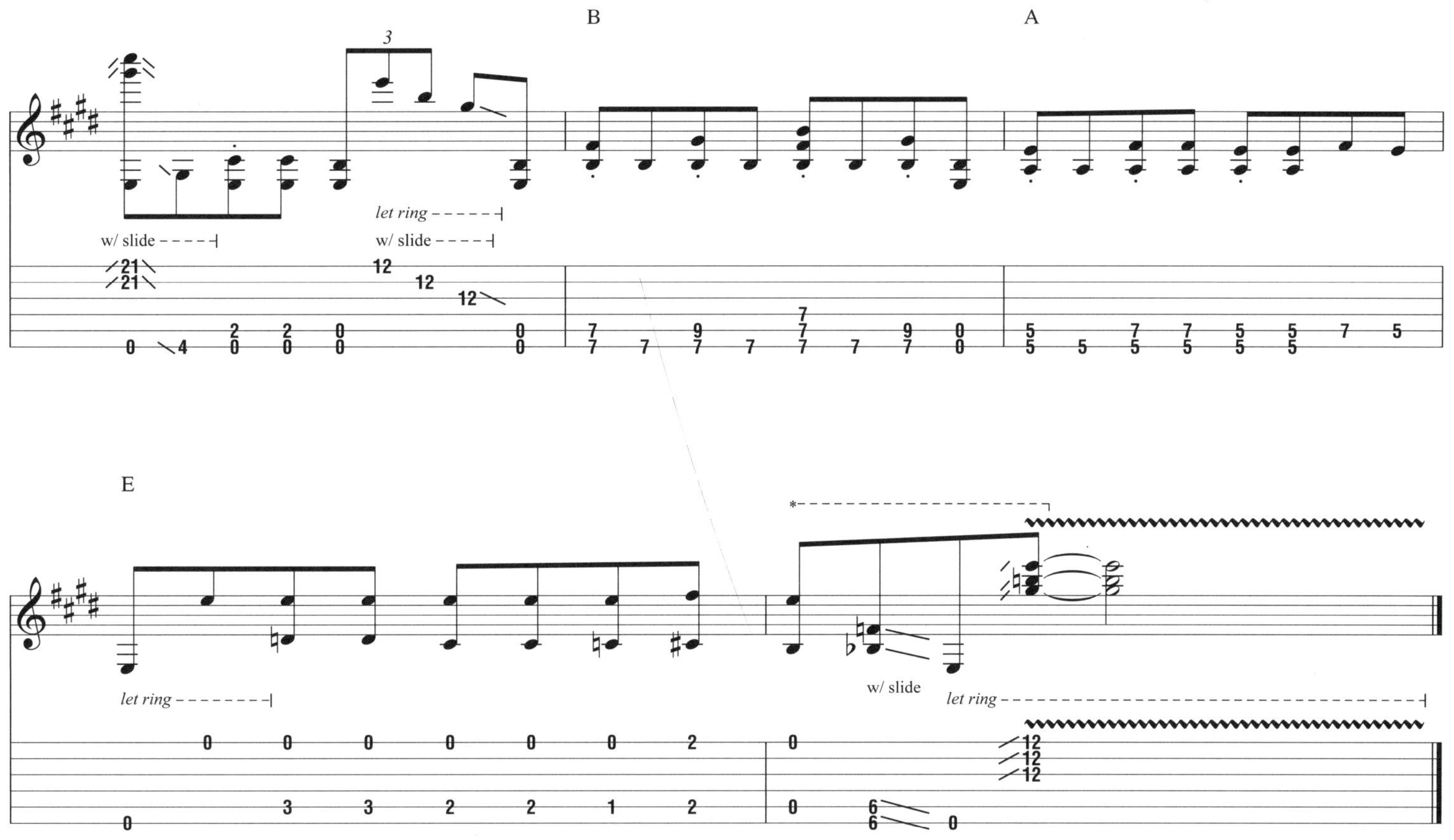

Blues Archaeology Though it is likely the E major triad played in triplets originated with piano players, the advantage on guitar is the sliding into the form from below, as expressed with great gusto by Bob in the video.

Open D

Open D is the same as open E except tuned one step down: low to high, D-A-D-F#-A-D. Singing in the high register of open E can be a strain at the top of the vocal range for some male singers. D is a full step lower, meaning less strain. Also, the whole guitar sound is lower in open D, and that feels good and full when you are playing solo or with a small band. A drawback is that you will have less tension on your strings when they're tuned lower. This can be an advantage for string bending if you were in standard tuning. For slide, less tension on the strings is a disadvantage. You're more likely to clank into the frets when you don't mean to as the strings bend easier into the neck under your slide. You can weigh the results of open E against open D depending on how it feels for your guitar. A change in tension may pull up or release the neck, though most solid body guitars are not so fragile for it to make much difference to the safety of the neck. The vocalist's preferred key and your own comfort with the tunings should help you decide which tuning to use. Great players choose D or E according to what feels and sounds right to them. You can, too.

Fig. 4: Open D tuning can be easier to sing with than E, and the higher slide notes are not as shrill as in open E. And that low D open note that I land on after "falling down the stairs" on the last lick is very dramatic.

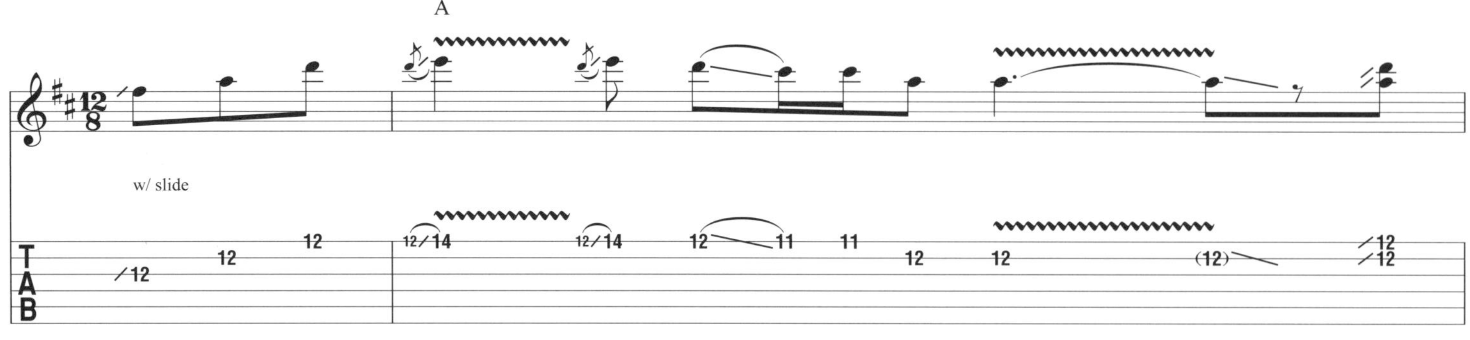

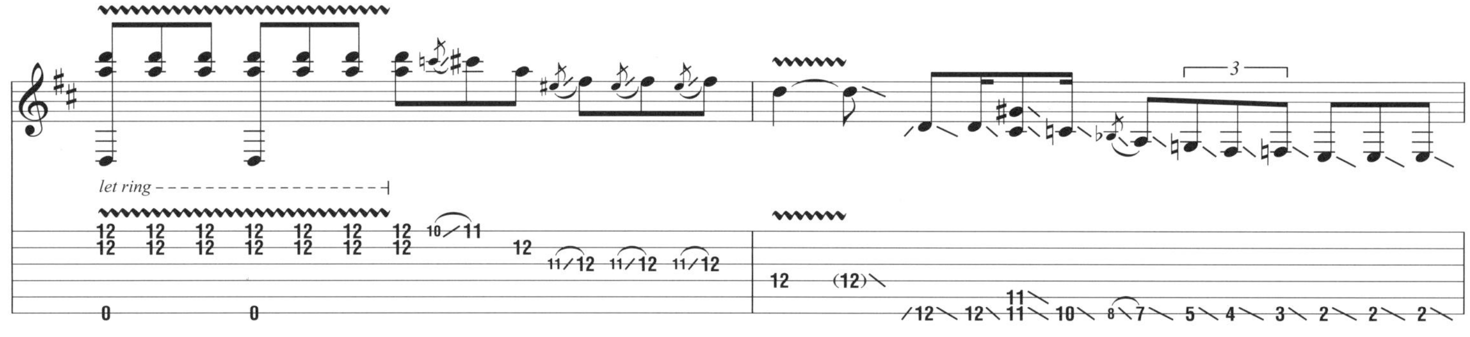

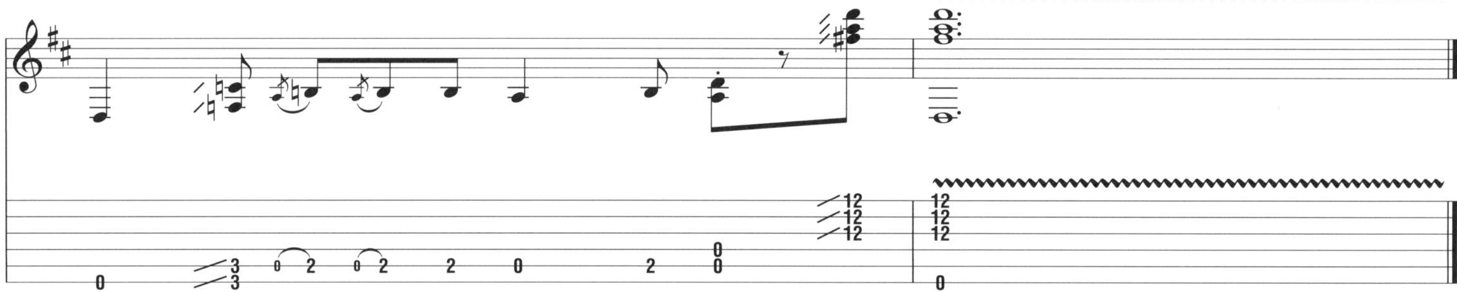

Blues Archaeology **Also known as "Vestapol," open D was one of the earliest open tunings used by guitar players in all styles in the late 1800s, before being appropriated by blues guitarists for slide.**

Open E Minor or D Minor

Tuning to open E minor from standard tuning is the same tuning as open E, except string 3 remains at G. In open D minor, string 3 is lowered one step to F. Minor keys impart a sad, eerie sound.

Fig. 5: An open D minor slow blues progression expressing sad sounds. The lower tonality, compared to open E minor, enhances it. If you want to hear the difference in that feeling, you can find a similar verse played in open E minor in **Fig. 58** at the end. Either way, the sound of minor open tunings is emotional. A bonus of open D minor slide guitar is that a chromatic harmonica, the large harp with a lever, is most often played in the key of D and the two of them together might break hearts.

Open Dm tuning:
(low to high) D-A-D-F-A-D

Moderately slow

Am Dm

w/ slide

let ring

Dm Gm

w/o slide

w/ slide

let ring

Dm Gm

w/o slide

let ring

w/ slide

w/o slide

let ring

w/ slide

Dm

let ring

Am Gm Dm

rit.

w/o slide

w/ slide

let ring

Blues Archaeology Amplified blues harmonica legend Little Walter Jacobs was known to play chromatic in minor keys on occasion. "Blue and Lonesome" in D minor is a good example, though his ace guitarist Luther Tucker is ripping in standard tuning with conventional fretting.

Open G

Open G tuning is as classic as open E. The sound of each can conjure traditional Delta blues or more modern creations. Open G could be the tuning of Son House, Robert Johnson, acoustic and electric Muddy Waters, or Keith Richards' creative extensions. The strings are tuned, low to high: D-G-D-G-B-D. The change from standard tuning is that the two lowest strings and the highest are tuned one step down. The first time you strum this open tuning, it just sounds good as a full, harmonious six-note chord. Start to slide around on the notes and you'll find you can play two or three together and they sound beautiful. Go up to the 12th fret and pick the highest three strings one at a time, high to low. You just played the opening signature lick of a famous open G classic.

Blues Archaeology Open G, also known as "Spanish," is probably the most popular tuning in all styles of guitar music.

You can also make chords with your fingers, without the slide, in open G. It is magical that chords you use in standard tuning sound exotic and bluesy when you play the same fingering in open G.

Fig. 6: An open G fingered lick that uses (what would be in standard tuning) a "baby" A minor chord. This lick slides on strings 3–1 at fret 12 and ends with a sustained vibrato note on string 1 at fret 5.

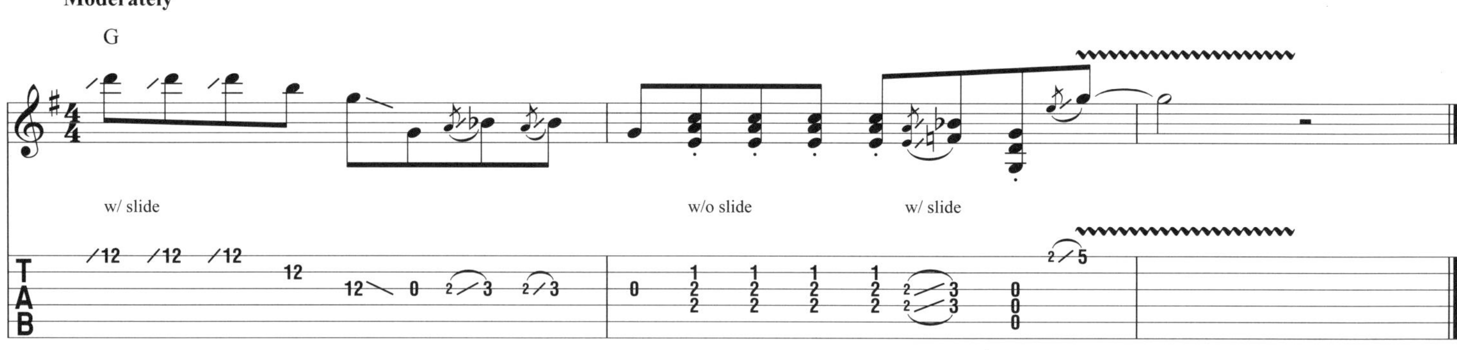

Blues Archaeology The Delta blues legend Son House was fond of open G. His "My Black Mama Pt. II" (1930) and its reworked version, recorded as "Death Letter Blues" (1965), are two of the most spellbinding slide guitar classics.

Fig. 7: A "baby" C chord in standard tuning becomes a menacing IV seventh chord when fingered in open G. Included are slide licks you can combine with that funky chord to play deep blues.

And of course, there are finger licks that are the standard ways to make non-slide chords in open G…

Fig. 8: An open G lick that sounds like an old car on a bumpy road. It's played on fret 5, and taking one finger on and off and back on again feels like driving. It is followed by a slide up to the single note G on fret 5 with vibrato.

Blues Archaeology **That bump or "chopping" rhythm is reminiscent of working songs known as "axe falls." Two men would swing axes on opposite sides of a tree or a log in a steady alternating rhythm, like down beats, so as not to chop each other.**

Open A

Open A is the same as open G except each string is tuned one step higher. Open A tuning is, low to high: E-A-E-A-C#-E. The higher tuning puts more tension on the strings, making them more taut and stable as you slide over them. And again, it raises the key if you're more comfortable singing a specific song in A rather than G. The playing technique is the same as open G, but there is a different tonality; the notes have a slightly different feeling to your ears than you would expect from just playing a step higher. With a larger band, Muddy preferred to play in open A rather than open G. His voice and guitar cut through better than if he were singing and playing in a lower key. However, solo or in a small ensemble, he usually used open G.

Blues Archaeology **Robert Johnson preferred open A (virtually always capoed to other keys) over open G, save for the open G, non-slide tune "Love in Vain Blues." Perhaps open A was used as a way to put his songs in keys more conducive to his vocal range and/or for the higher string tension.**

Open G Minor or Open A Minor

In open G minor, string 2 (B) is tuned down a half step to B♭. In open A minor, it is tuned up a half step to C. Strum the strings of the open chord and it will give you chills. I first heard this tuning on a 1994 Muddy Waters collection, *One More Mile*, which included a Swiss radio recording of Muddy playing in open G minor by himself. We will explore this intriguing tuning in the Muddy section of this book and in my Master Class in Chapter IX.

Other Open Tunings

In the mid-1970s, Muddy did some club shows in Denver with Geoff Muldaur opening. He is such a great singer that it is easy to forget he's a very advanced and creative guitar player. Hanging in the dressing room one night, he showed me an open C tuning. I don't remember what the notes were, but the E string tuned down two full steps to C was a very low note to be coming out of a six-string guitar. He played a little bit and open C sounded like a different voicing from anything I had heard before. The point is not to learn open C. I am sure it has been discussed and analyzed and explained elsewhere. But traditional open tunings can be the foundation of a player's signature style or just the jumping-off point for a musical trip to outer or inner space. Experiment with different tunings! Invent one and learn how to find some exotic sounds, slide guitar or not. The "final chapter" completing the "book of slide guitar" has not been written yet.

CHAPTER II:
Acoustic Chicago Blues in the 1940s

Chicago in the 1940s could claim an urbane musical environment that boasted (besides Big Bill Broonzy and Memphis Minnie) one of the most accomplished bottleneck guitarists in Hudson "Tampa Red" Woodbridge Whittaker. He performed "hokum," or novelty numbers, as well as traditional blues, and today is acknowledged for his melodic bottleneck work.

Likewise, Robert Lee "Robert Nighthawk" McCollum McCoy was setting high standards and is a link between prewar acoustic bottleneck and postwar electric slide guitar. Bob Margolin comments that, "I love his wide, deep vibrato which echoes the vibrato of his voice." His slide songs are moody and remarkable for their nuanced clarity and lack of unwanted dissonance endemic to standard-tuned slide. Bob also recalls, "Muddy said Nighthawk played at his first wedding in Mississippi and people danced so hard Muddy thought the floor might cave in. I think Muddy was influenced by Nighthawk, after Robert Johnson and Son House."

(**Note:** Robert Nighthawk's career spanned several decades from prewar to postwar. However, his most famous and influential playing was in the latter and for that reason he is covered in Chapter IV.)

Tampa Red (1904–1981)

Hudson "Tampa Red" Whittaker (born Woodbridge in Tampa, Florida) was one of the charter members of the prewar Chicago blues community, revered for his exceptional single-string slide guitar work. His long, extremely prolific recording career began in 1928 with "It's Tight Like That," a risqué tune in the popular double entendre "hokum" style. He often performed and recorded with Thomas A. "Georgia Tom" Dorsey as the Hokum Boys, as well as with Frankie Jaxon as Tampa Red's Hokum Jug Band. By the 1930s, his virtuosic riffs and solos earned him the moniker the "Guitar Wizard," and he became a sought-after session musician playing behind Ma Rainey, Sonny Boy Williamson, Memphis Minnie, Big Maceo Merriweather, and many others. In the 1940s, he was picking electric guitar, including on "Crying Won't Help You" (1946) with Big Maceo on piano, though his first, upbeat version of "It Hurts Me, Too" was cut acoustically in 1940. In 1949, he redid it more somberly as "When Things Go Wrong with You" in a combo with his kazoo solos. Unfortunately, after recording in 1961, he quit playing and his last years were lived out in poor health.

Fig. 9: Fast blues, Tampa Red-style in open D, slowed down. He had an instantly recognizable slide style.

Open D tuning:
(low to high) D-A-D-F♯-A-D

Moderately

D7

w/ slide

w/o slide

G7

D7

A7

D7

let ring

w/ slide

Fig. 10: Tampa Red-style slow blues in open D. The fretted chord changes for his IV and V chords are part of the classic Tampa Red sound.

Open D tuning:
(low to high) D-A-D-F♯-A-D

Moderately

D

w/ slide

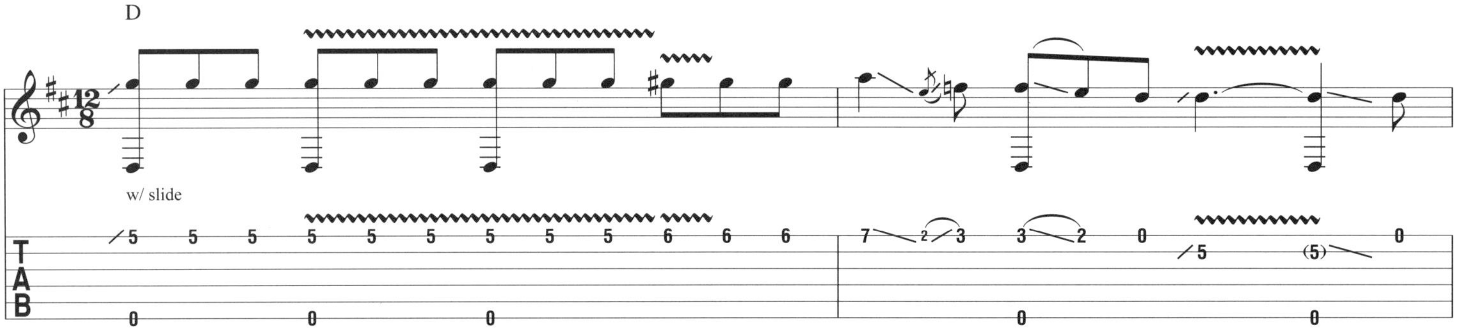

Blues Archaeology Tampa Red was arguably the first blues guitarist to buy a National Steel Resonator in 1928, the first year of manufacture. The increased volume of his fancy Tricone model allowed his famous single-note lines to be better heard in performance and on recordings.

CHAPTER III:
The 1950s

Elmore James (1918–1963)

"Elmo" James is roundly acknowledged as the "King of Electric Slide Guitar." The musical heir of Kokomo Arnold, Robert Johnson, and Tampa Red, he established an instantly recognizable style created from a set number of riffs he recycled and manipulated. His recording career began in 1951, when he backed Sonny Boy Williamson II and Willie Love. In 1952, his debut as a leader was spectacular with the release of the landmark "Dust My Broom" (#9 R&B). The signature riff, based on Robert Johnson's fretted "(I Believe) I'll Dust My Broom," is one of the most copied in blues and rock history while copyright ownership of the song has been disputed. In the ensuing 12 years, he also contributed to the postwar blues canon with the classics "It Hurts Me, Too," "The Sky Is Crying," "Shake Your Moneymaker," and "Something Inside Me," among others, often with the inestimable backing of unsung blues guitar hero Eddie Taylor. The Allman Brothers recorded his "Done Somebody Wrong" and Jimi Hendrix recorded live versions of "Bleeding Heart."

Fig. 11: Four measures in the shuffle style of Elmore James. This lick declares "Chicago Blues."

Open D tuning:
(low to high) D-A-D-F♯-A-D

Moderately

D

w/ slide

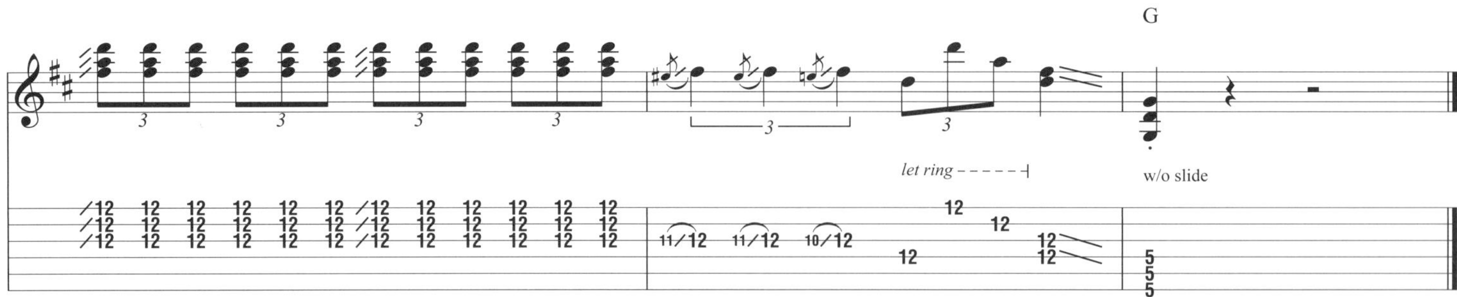

Fig. 12: This shuffle style of Elmore James delivers the classic lick first and then some picking of individual notes to elaborate on it.

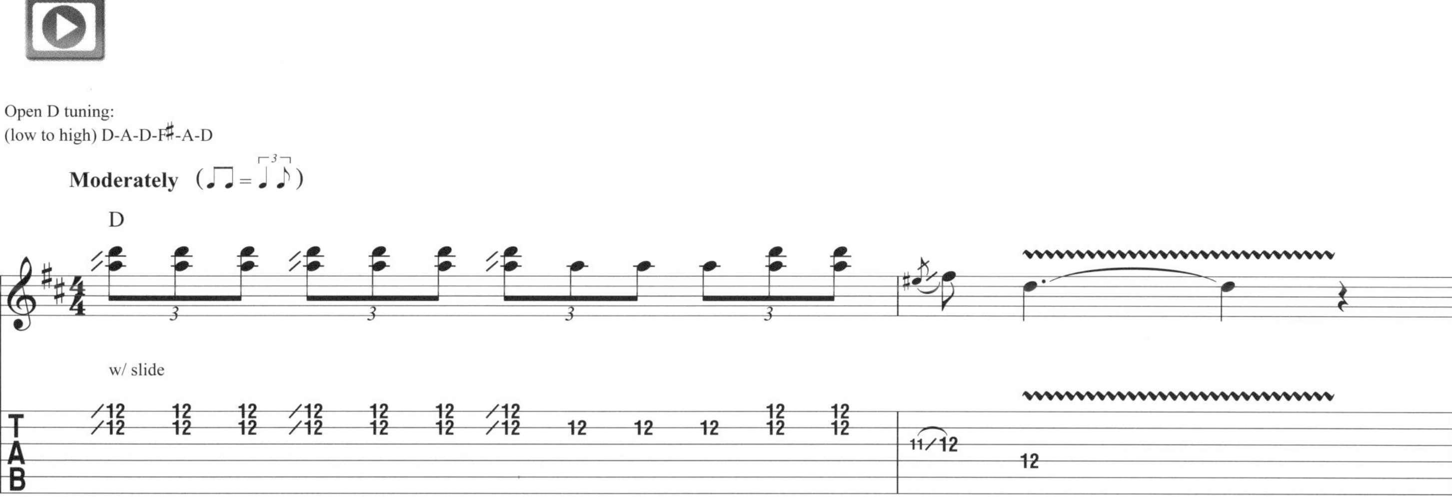

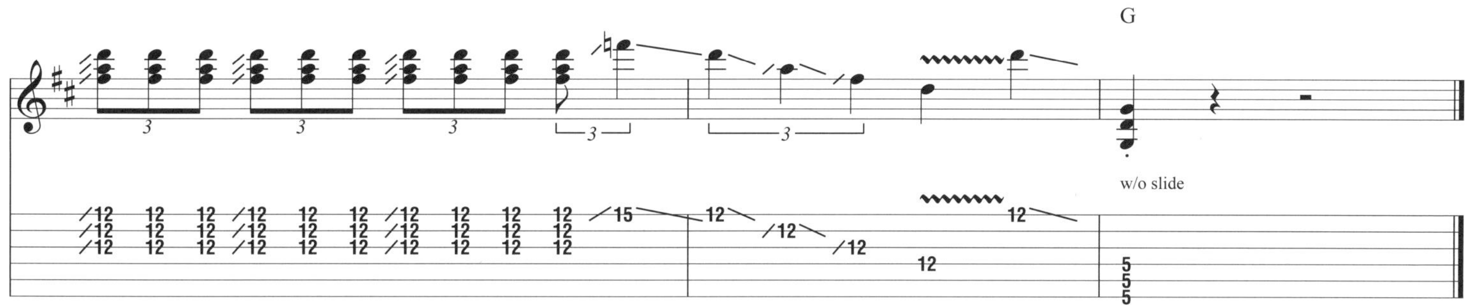

Fig. 13: Twelve measures of a shuffle in the style of an Elmore James classic. The melody is similar to one he was known to sing.

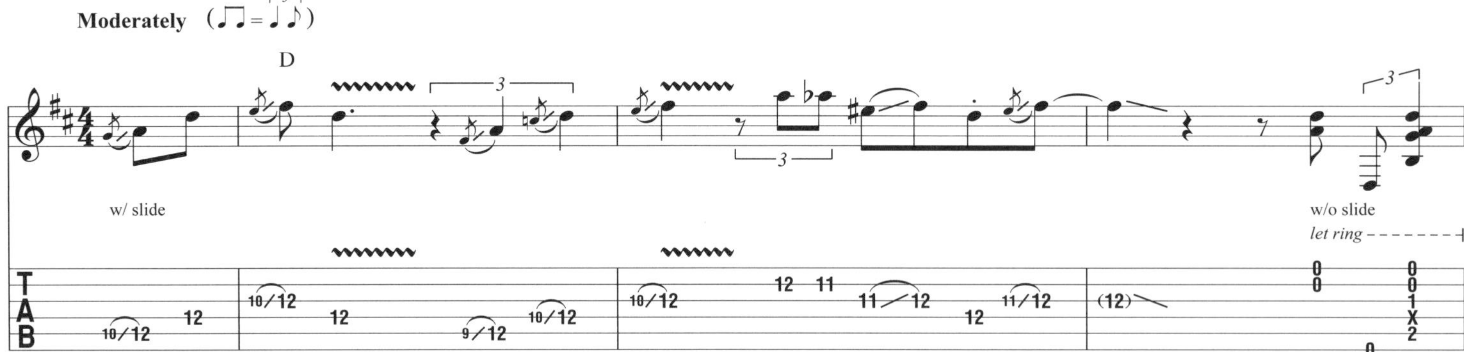

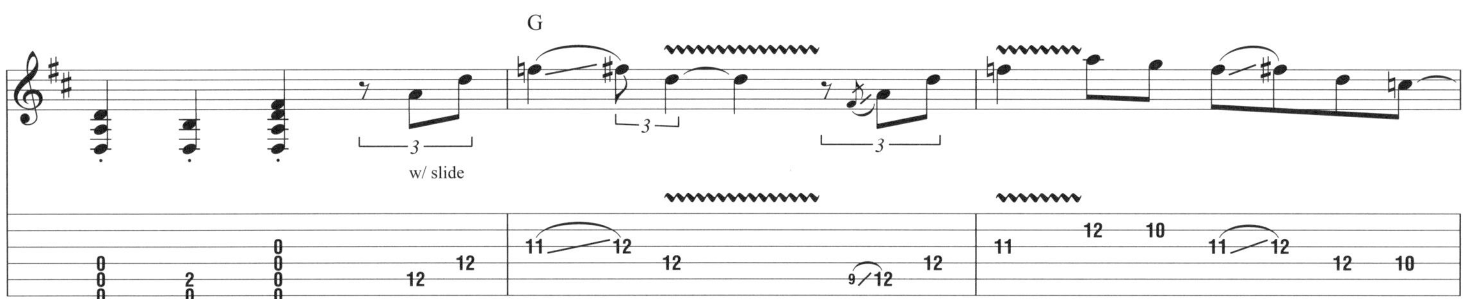

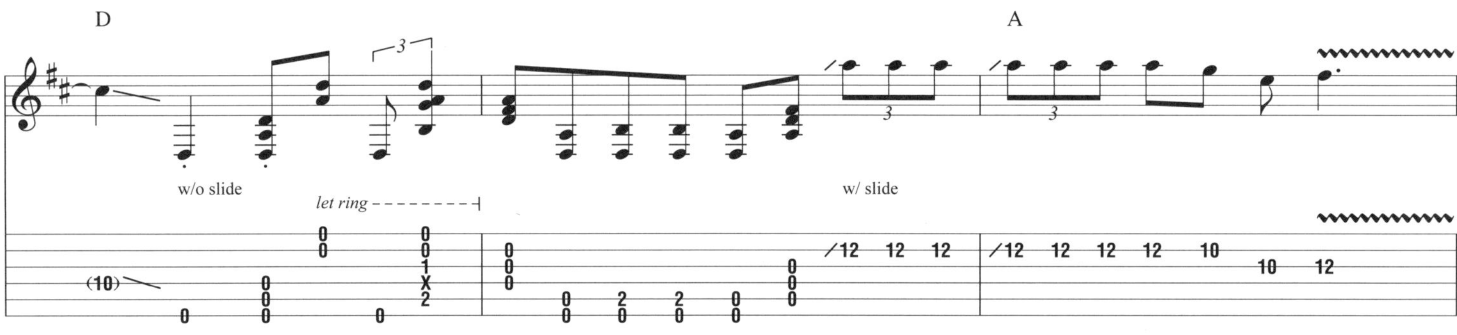

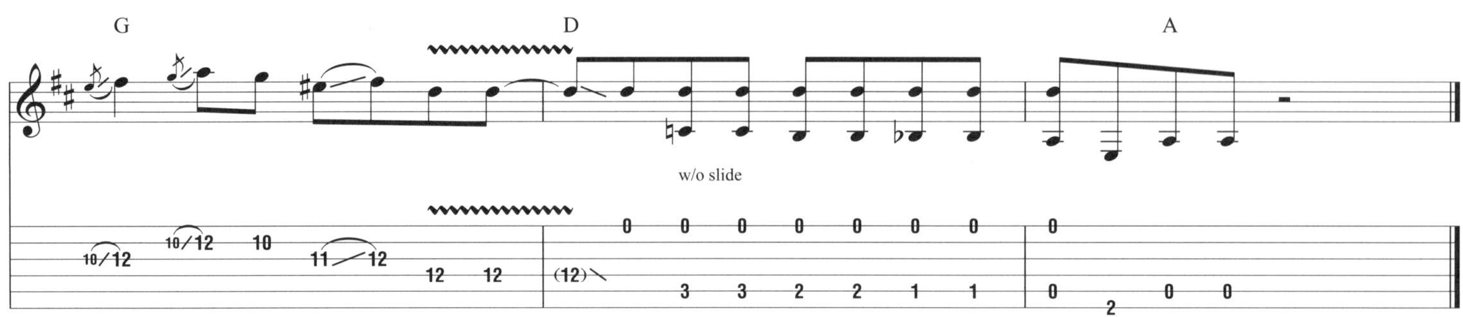

Fig. 14: Four measures of an Elmore James-style intro and ending. Note how little hesitations and slides impart a bluesy feeling.

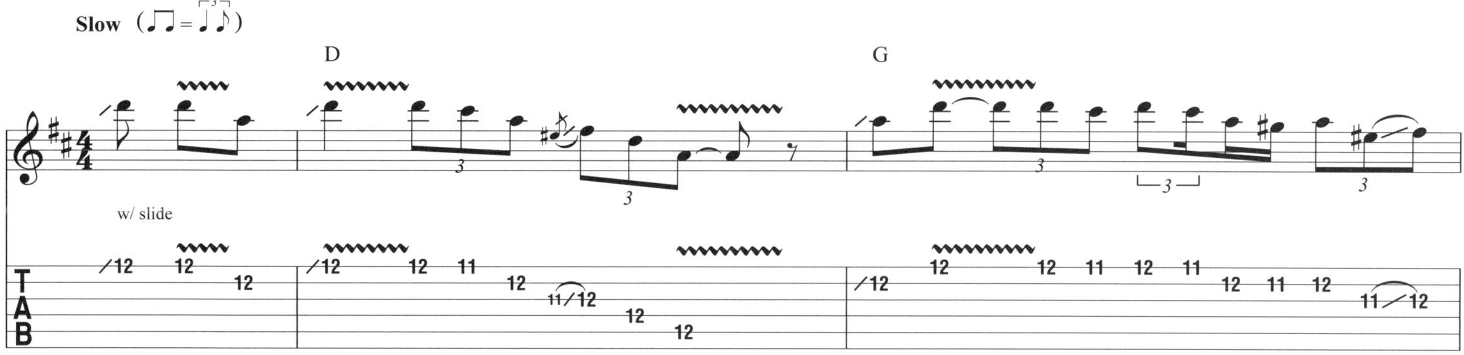

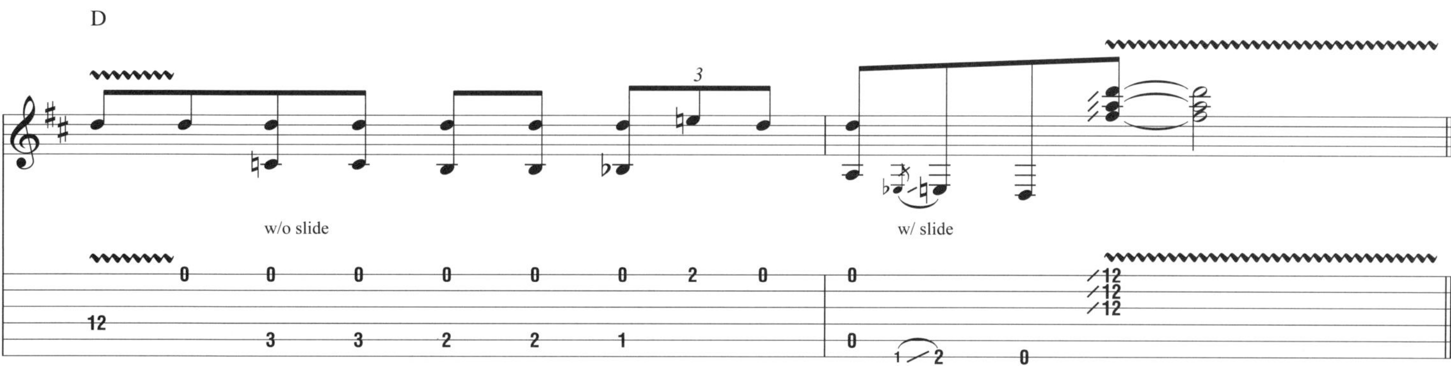

Blues Archaeology Erotic topics, often expressed with humorous double entendres, have long been a staple of blues lyrics. When combined with a suggestive shuffle beat, the result is timeless appeal up to the present day.

Fig. 15: Two 12-measure verses of up-tempo blues in the style of Elmore James. There are little embellishments and fast accents that can be added, but this is basic.

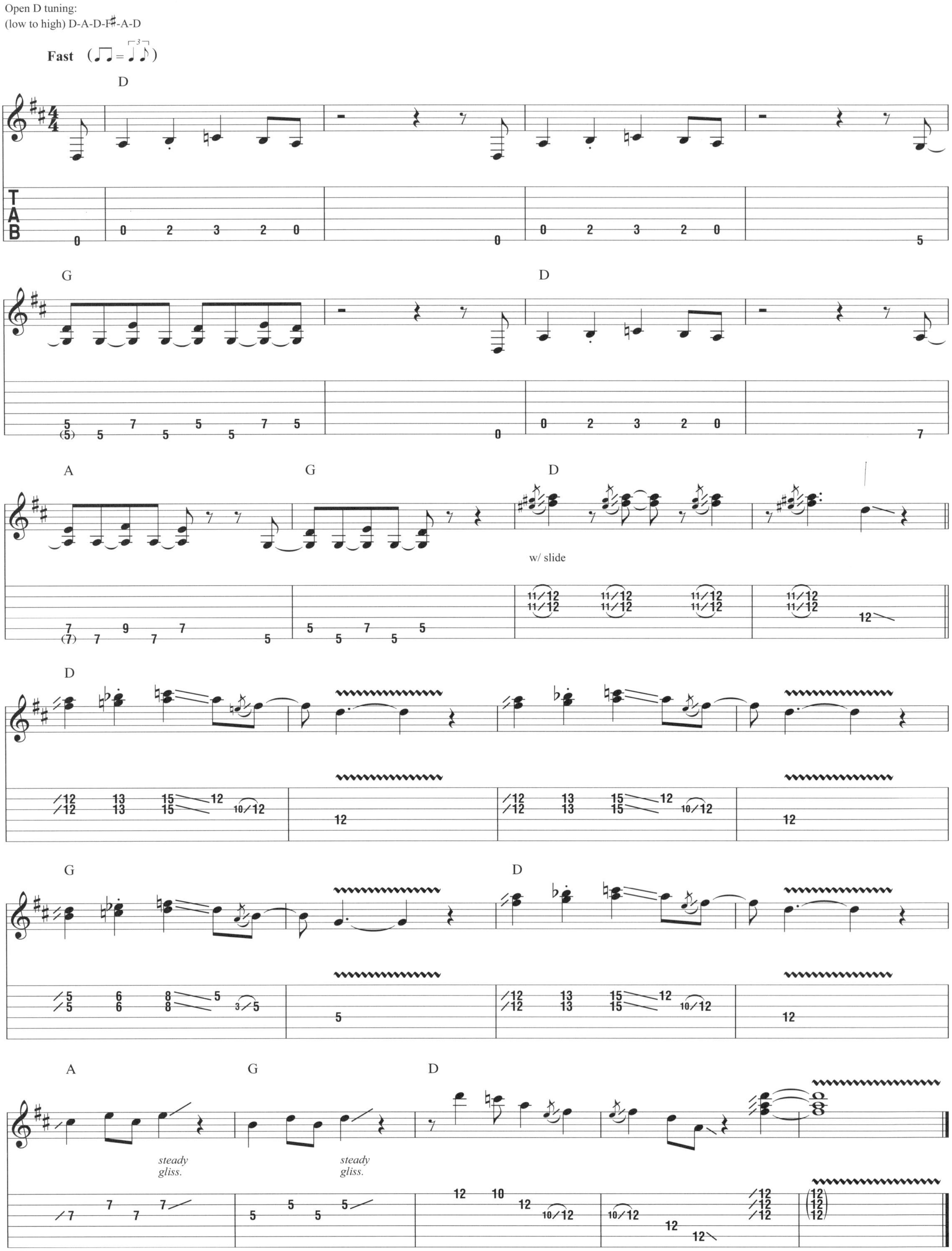

Open D tuning:
(low to high) D-A-D-F♯-A-D

Fast

D G D A G D

w/ slide

steady gliss.

steady gliss.

Fig. 16: Two 12-measure verses as in **Fig. 15** but played more slowly and applied to a swinging shuffle. Sounds good at this tempo and is easier to learn. **Fig. 15** is intense; this one is slinkier.

Open D tuning:
(low to high) D-A-D-F♯-A-D

Moderately (♫ = ♩♪ triplet)

D

G D

A G D

w/ slide

D

G D

A G D

steady gliss. *steady gliss.*

Fig. 17: Eight-bar, slow- to medium-tempo blues in the style of Elmore James. So simple, but play the notes with a slight hesitation as though they are words that almost hurt you too much to say.

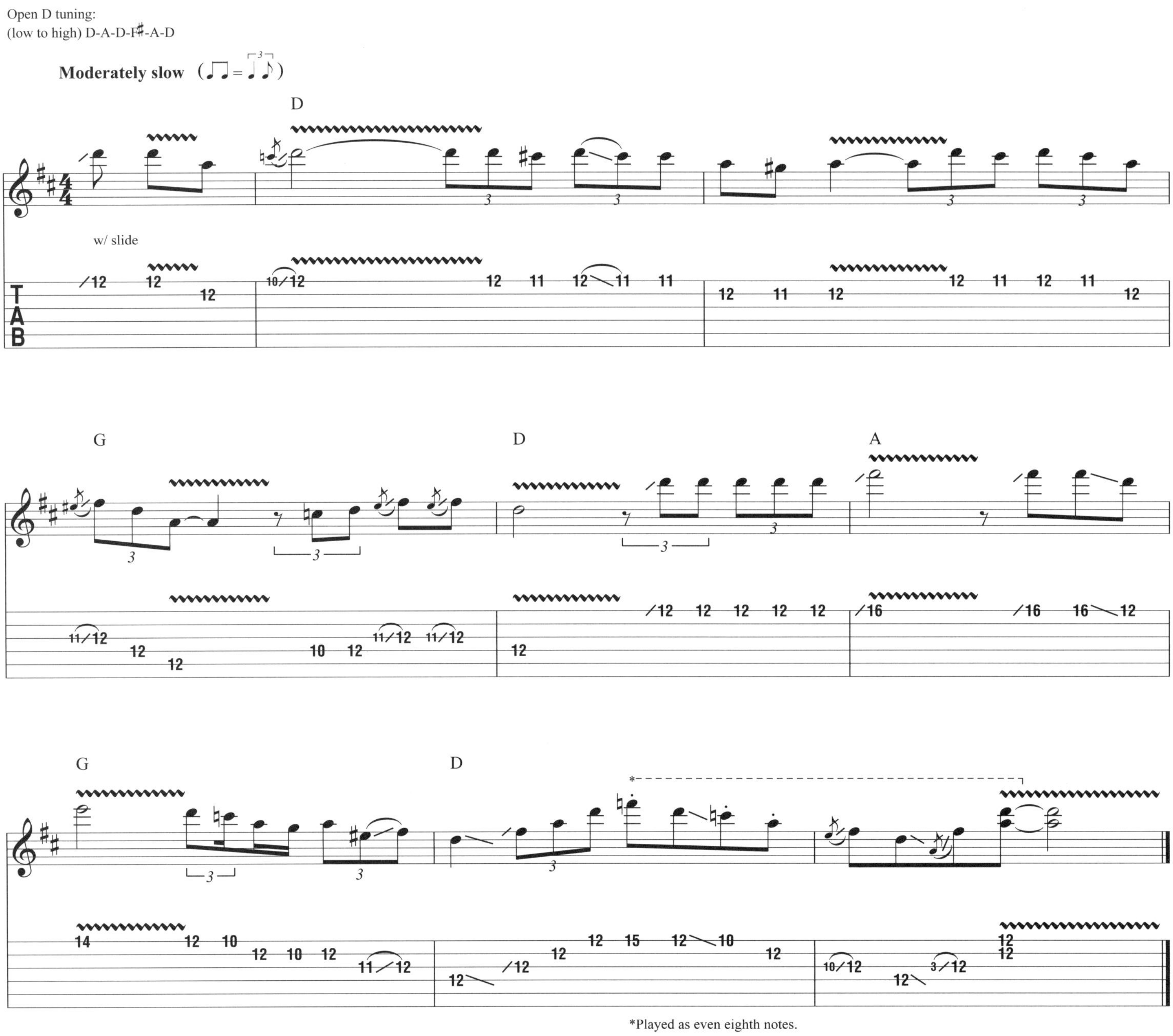

Open D tuning:
(low to high) D-A-D-F♯-A-D

Moderately slow

D

w/ slide

G D A

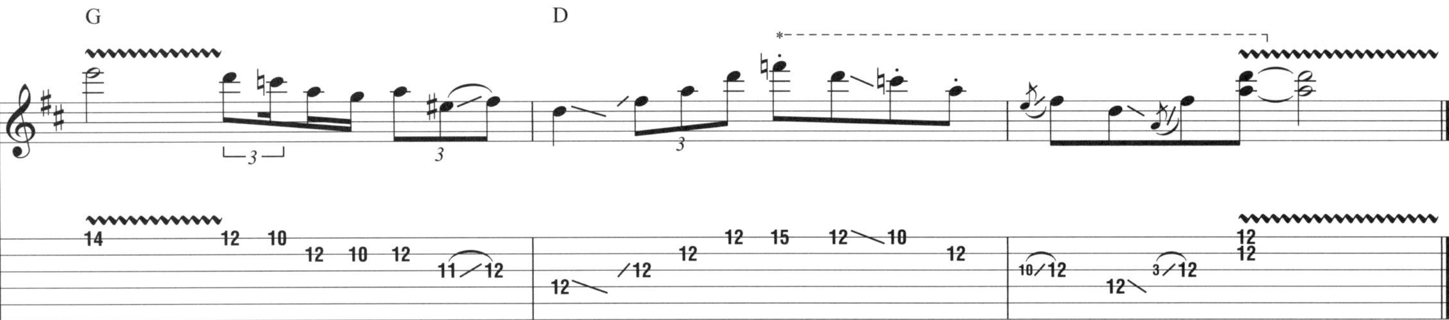

*Played as even eighth notes.

Blues Archaeology The expression of longing, heartache, or mourning has long been a prime expression of slide guitar. Proof goes back at least as far as 1903 when W.C. Handy heard the lonely slide guitarist accompanying his singing of "Goin' Where the Southern Cross the Dog," a reference to two prominent train lines in Mississippi.

Howlin' Wolf (1910–1976)

Along with his contemporary blues immortal, Muddy Waters, Chester Arthur "Howlin' Wolf" Burnett had the most commanding presence in postwar blues. He was and is instantly recognized by his vocal growl and "howl," though he was an incisive guitarist and harmonica player, too. He learned the former from none other than Charley Patton, the "Father of Delta Blues," in the 1930s and was a performer throughout the decade with his peers Johnny Shines, Honeyboy Edwards, Robert Johnson, Robert Lockwood, Jr., and Son House. By the early 1950s, he was recording "How Many More Years" b/w "Moaning at Midnight" for Sam Phillips in Memphis, and then had his contract bought by Chess Records in Chicago where he would move. "Who Will Be Next," "Smokestack Lightning," and "I Asked for Water (She Gave Me Gasoline)" were also R&B hits in the 1950s, while "Wang Dang Doodle," "Back Door Man," "Spoonful," "Little Red Rooster," "I Ain't Superstitious," "Goin' Down Slow," and "Killing Floor" followed in the 1960s. Over the years, he had many of the best blues guitarists at his side, including Willie Johnson, Matt "Guitar" Murphy, Pat Hare, Jody Williams, and particularly Hubert Sumlin, who would stay with him from the mid-1950s for virtually the rest of his career. Wolf played slide guitar on some of his recordings and live performances in open G style, notably "Meet Me in the Bottom" and the famous blues standard, "Little Red Rooster."

Blues Archaeology Two Delta classics from 1929, Patton's "Down the Dirt Road Blues" and Blind Willie Newbern's "Roll and Tumble Blues," prefigure crucial elements in Wolf's own significant contribution to the blues canon.

Fig. 18: In the style of a Howlin' Wolf classic. Howlin' Wolf was probably inspired by Charley Patton for this groove. Played faster, these licks sound like an old train going fast.

Open G tuning:
(low to high) D-G-D-G-B-D

Moderately

G

w/ slide

steady gliss.

let ring

C

G

steady gliss.

let ring

D

C

G

Blues Archaeology The sound produced by locomotives figure prominently in the development of blues guitar. "Cut boogie" rhythm patterns are evocative of chugging steam engines, while the slide can be used to imitate the sound of a wailing train whistle relatively easily.

Johnny Shines (1915–1992)

Perhaps unfairly known mainly for just being the "running buddy" of Robert Johnson, Johnny Shines was an exceptionally skilled country blues guitarist who rightfully belongs in the company of his more esteemed fellow bluesmen. He began playing guitar in Memphis around 16 or 17, turned professional in 1932, and "rambled" with Johnson from 1935–1937. In 1941, he moved to Chicago, but by 1946, a lengthy period of frustration with the music business commenced, following small electric combo recordings for Columbia Records which were not released. The same thing happened at Chess Records in 1950. In 1952, he recorded what is considered his best work for J.O.B. Records, but it failed to sell in quantity. Giving up, he pawned his gear and went back to working construction jobs into the 1960s. However, in 1966 he was "discovered" taking photographs in a Chicago blues club and it led to him recording six tracks for the modern classic *Chicago/The Blues/Today! Vol. 3*. Concerts, tours (including with Robert Lockwood, Jr.), and numerous recordings would keep him playing even as he moved to Alabama in 1969. His Testament, Rounder, and Blind Pig records, in particular, show him to be an unquestioned Delta blues master, and his solo songs reveal him to be the greatest interpreter of Robert Johnson. In 1980, he suffered a stroke which curtailed his career until around 1989. Unfortunately, the subsequent recordings from that point to his death only contain his vocals, as he could no longer play guitar up to his expectations.

Blues Archaeology **Johnny Shines once stated that he and Robert Johnson played Kalamazoo archtop guitars. However, photographic evidence shows Johnson with a Gibson L-1 flattop in the pinstripe suit studio shot, and a Kalamazoo KG-14 in the photo booth picture with the cigarette, as well as the photo booth picture recently revealed by his stepsister Annye C. Anderson. Ms. Anderson came to a Muddy Waters show in Boston in 1978 and brought the two famous photos to show to Muddy. She asked Bob Margolin to bring her backstage to meet Muddy between sets. When she showed Muddy the photos, he said he had not ever seen Robert in Mississippi, though he was one of his biggest influences, along with Son House. Muddy said he tried once to see Robert, but it was too crowded and he couldn't get in.**

Fig. 19: One chorus of classic Johnny Shines-style blues using both fingers and slide in open G. The notes are more melodic than some Delta blues-inspired rhythms and they are played with the slide over fret 12, just as they lay in that tuning.

Open G tuning:
(low to high) D-G-D-G-B-D

Moderately (♫ = ♩ ♪ triplet)

G

w/ slide

C

D

G

Honeyboy Edwards (1915–2011)

David "Honeyboy" Edwards acquired his nickname while trying to walk as a toddler and his sisters said, "Aw, look at Honey, Mama, look at little Honey." When he died, David "Honeyboy" Edwards had been the last living link back to the Delta blues era. Drawn to the blues life early on, he headed out on the Southern byways with Big Joe Williams at the age of 14 for six months and would remain on the road through to the 1940s. He claimed to have been with Robert Johnson the day he died in 1938. In 1942, ethno-music researcher Alan Lomax recorded 15 songs with Edwards in Clarksdale, Mississippi, for the Library of Congress. It would be nearly a decade later that he made his first commercial recordings for the ARC label when he moved to Chicago. His "Drop Down Mama" for Chess Records from 1953 is a classic example of Delta bottleneck guitar and one of his most well-known compositions, but his recorded output through the 1950s and 1960s consisted of less than 10 sides. His first LP, *I've Been Around*, a collection of tracks from the early 1970s, was released in 1978. From 1980 on, his association with Earwig Records in Chicago resulted in a handful of records while he also cut tracks for various other labels. In 1997, his autobiography *The World Don't Owe Me Nothing: The Life and Times of Bluesman Honeyboy Edwards* was published. He would continue to perform, even if sporadically, virtually up to his death. In 2008, Edwards made an instructional DVD for Hal Leonard called *Delta Blues Guitar*.

Blues Archaeology **By recorded evidence, most prewar blues slide guitarists played in open tunings as it complimented their solo chordal accompaniment style. However, slide in standard has advantages, including offering a different gritty sound and style, while also allowing conventional fretting and standard chord forms.**

Fig. 20: One chorus of classic Honeyboy Edwards-style in standard tuning, showing both slide and fingering techniques. He would take classic open-tuning slide licks and play them with a slide in standard tuning.

Moderately slow (♫ = ♩♪ triplet)

E

w/ slide

w/ slide

A

w/ slide

w/ slide

E

B

w/ slide

A

E Am/E C♯°/E

let ring

E7 B

let ring

Earl Hooker (1930–1970)

The legendary Earl Zebedee Hooker moved with his family from Mississippi to Chicago the year of his birth and heard music in his home growing up. John Lee Hooker was a cousin. By 1942, he was playing on street corners with friends, including Bo Diddley, while coming under the influence of the swinging blues guitar of T-Bone Walker. He met and befriended Robert Nighthawk, who shared his slide guitar technique with the younger man. Hooker went to Arkansas in 1946, where he played with Nighthawk and Sonny Boy Williamson II for a number of years before settling back down in Chicago in the early 1950s, in between bouts of touring the South. He began recording mostly as an instrumentalist, as his vocals were considered weak. Hooker was house guitarist for Chief Records from 1959–1963, backing a bevy of Chicago luminaries including Junior Wells. In 1961, before a session, his warm-up—a slow slide blues instrumental—was surreptitiously taped by record label owner Mel London and later released to acclaim as "Blue Guitar." In 1962, Leonard Chess wanted to use it as a backing track for a Muddy Waters song with lyrics by Willie Dixon, which would become the classic "You Shook Me." The collaboration was so successful that three more of Hooker's instrumentals were given lyrics for Muddy to sing, including "You Need Love." He continued recording, performing, and touring (including a jaunt to England) literally up until his death from complications of tuberculosis, which had plagued him for most of his life.

Blues Archaeology Many fans believe Earl Hooker was the greatest Chicago blues guitarist. Arguably, his virtuosic skills, both fretting and playing slide, confirms the veracity of the statement.

Fig. 21: Slow blues intro and progression using slide and conventional fretting in the style of Earl Hooker. Earl had a proficiency and intensity that made other great players admire and respect him. Pinetop Perkins, who played piano with him for a while, told me that Earl Hooker played so loud onstage that "he deefed me!" and lost some of the hearing in the ear near Earl's amp.

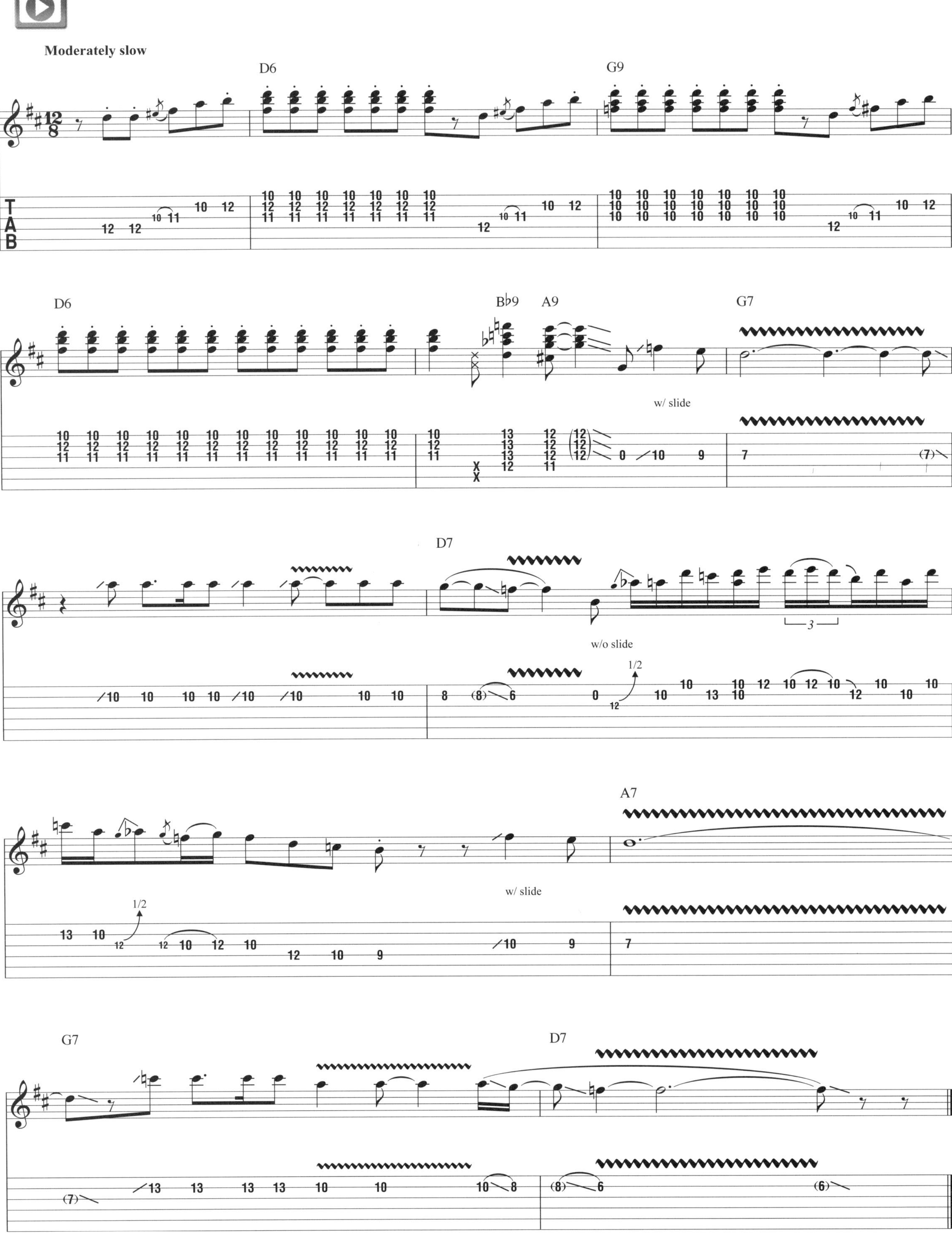

CHAPTER IV:
The 1960s

Robert Nighthawk (1909–1967)

Robert Lee "Robert Nighthawk" McCollum, known as "Prowling Nighthawk" for his song of the same name, as well as "Robert Lee McCoy," remains near-mythical despite having lived into the latter 20th century. Indeed, he was even interviewed for posterity by Michael Bloomfield in 1964. His penchant for "prowling," or rambling, may have been due in part to a scrape with the law regarding a pistol. In the mid-1920s, he played harmonica in the South, picking up the guitar around 1930. He appears to have learned slide from Eugene "Sonny Boy Nelson" Powell and began recording on acoustic guitar in the mid-1930s through 1940. He always returned to his home town of Helena, Arkansas, though also spent time in Chicago in the 1940s, where he became one of the first blues guitarists to play electric slide. While there, he came under the influence of Tampa Red, who he was known to imitate on occasion. "Sweet Black Angel" (1956), later made into a hit by B.B. King as "Sweet Little Angel," was a signature song, and his *Live on Maxwell Street* (1963) is prized by blues guitarists for his scorching tone.

Blues Archaeology **Long before distortion stomp boxes were manufactured to achieve overdriven tones in the 1960s, electric blues guitarists discovered and utilized the expressive possibilities of tube amps pushed to the limits. One of the earliest to "catch lightning (and thunder) in a bottle" was Eddie "Guitar Slim" Jones on his classic "The Things I Used to Do" (1954), "The Story of My Life," and others.**

Fig. 22: Two verses of Robert Nighthawk-style slide in standard tuning. Robert was also very accomplished playing in standard tuning without a slide. And he did not "go electric" meekly when he got to Chicago, where he used small amplifiers cranked.

B
E
A
E
B
A
E
E6
steady gliss.

J.B. Hutto (1926–1983)

Joseph Benjamin "J.B." Hutto was born in South Carolina where he sang gospel with his brothers and sisters. The family moved to Chicago in 1949 where he would first play drums and piano before switching to guitar as one of Elmore James' many disciples. He formed a band called the Hawks, the nickname for the cold wind which blows off the lake in Chicago, performing in clubs and recording three singles in 1954, including the exceedingly raw and basic slow blues "Now She's Gone" and the salacious "Pet Cream Man" that was actually banned by one DJ. However, from the mid-1950s to the mid-1960s, he became discouraged and gave up music to work in a funeral home. Like Johnny Shines, he had the good fortune to appear on *Chicago/The Blues/Today! Vol. 1*, thereby resuscitating his career. The lauded "Hawk Squat!" in 1968 established him as a slide guitarist to be reckoned with on the Chicago scene. When Hound Dog Taylor died in 1976, Hutto took over his Houserockers, a band of guitar and drums. Though never recording commercially, the intensity of their live shows was something to behold. The same year, Hutto relocated to Boston with a New Hawks, recording and touring the US and Europe until his death.

Fig. 23: Slow blues intro in open E tuning. J.B. really enjoyed the "slide" part of playing slide guitar, adding those expressive, quick slides up or down from the main notes he hit, as though he was asking a question with "up" and declaring something with "down."

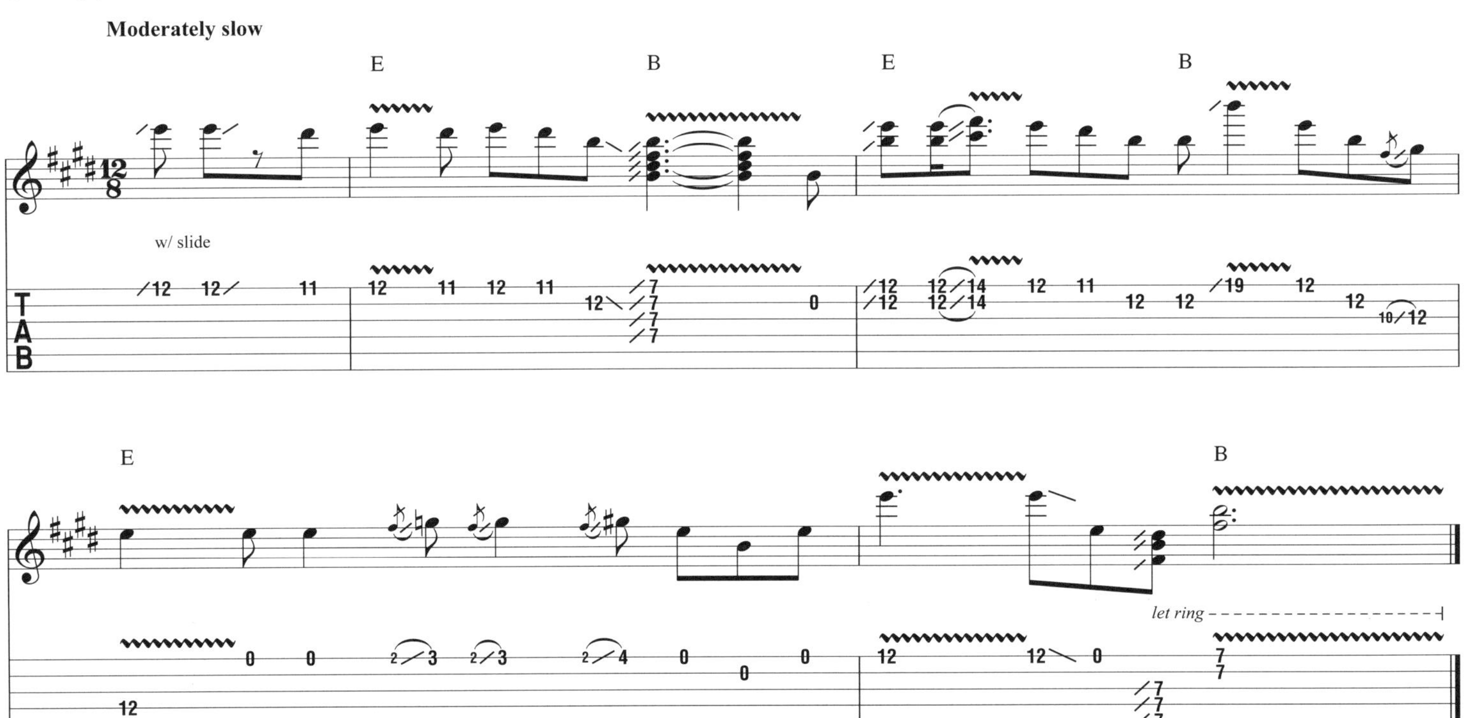

Blues Archaeology **Sliding into the intended note from below or above represents the unique, "organic" nature of the blues, acknowledged as a derivative of "field hollers" and other early African-American vocal styles.**

CHAPTER V:
The 1970s

Hound Dog Taylor (1915–1975)

Theodore Roosevelt "Hound Dog" Taylor epitomized post-Elmore James Chicago slide guitar at its most basic and grittiest. Born in Mississippi, where he began playing guitar in 1935, Taylor moved to Chicago in 1942, making the migration in the early 1940s, as did so many other African Americans during the WWII era. By 1957, he was gigging full time in the clubs, and ten years later, toured Europe with the American Folk Blues Festival. The big break came in 1971 when Taylor and his Houserockers were heard by Bruce Iglauer, who would go on to found Alligator records with the express purpose of recording the band. *Hound Dog Taylor and the Houserockers*, featuring drummer Ted Harvey and Brewer Phillips on lead guitar and de facto bass, was well-received in 1971. The loud and raucous recording essentially reproduced the sound of the band rocking a small club and was like a punch in the ear to the blues community. Unfortunately, only two more would follow in Taylor's lifetime, though several posthumous releases have added to his legacy. Taylor himself summed it up best when he said he wanted his epitaph to be, "He couldn't play shit, but he sure made it sound good."

Fig. 24: Eight bars of attitude in open E tuning. Hound Dog picked hard and percussively, and his phrasing pounded home the groove—no hesitations.

Open E tuning:
(low to high) E-B-E-G♯-B-E

Moderately

Fig. 25: Two-beat shuffle groove in open D. This shows how Hound Dog used quick slides up or down at the end of his slide notes and could also just fret a lick on the high strings, simple and strong.

Open D tuning:
(low to high) D-A-D-F♯-A-D

Fast

D

w/ slide

G

w/o slide

D

w/ slide

w/o slide

A

G

D

w/ slide

Homesick James (1910–2006)

Born John A. Williamson in Tennessee, possibly in 1905, he taught himself to play guitar at 10 and would be influenced by Blind Blake, Robert Johnson, and Elmore James—whom he claimed as his cousin and for whom he bought a guitar and taught to play. Williamson ran away from home and "rambled" through the South from the age of 14, meeting Yank Rachell, Sleepy John Estes, Blind Boy Fuller, and Big Joe Turner in the 1920s before moving to Chicago around 1930. He first recorded in 1937 for RCA Victor and began playing electric guitar a year later. From the late 1940s into the 1950s, he worked with Sonny Boy Williamson II, Elmore James, Baby Face Leroy Foster, Snooky Pryor, and others. He cut some of his best music for Chance Records in 1952–1953, including his classic "Homesick" from whence he acquired his nickname. From 1955–1963, he was a member of Elmore James' Broomdusters as a performer and recording sideman, and it is believed Elmore died of a heart attack in Williamson's apartment in 1963. He picked up his solo career and released a lauded album, *Blues on the South Side*, in 1964 on Prestige Records, containing one of his best-known tracks, "Gotta Move." In 1965, he was included on the landmark series *Chicago/The Blues/Today!* Williamson would release 14 more albums through to 2003. He remains unjustly neglected, perhaps because he was more known for his Robert Johnson covers than his originals.

Blues Archaeology He will always be tied to Elmore James, but Homesick James got out from underneath that all-encompassing shadow, as proved by the well-crafted chordal riffs on "Gotta Move."

Fig. 26: Two verses in the style of Homesick James. Homesick played expressively but simply. These verses are presented without second guitar to show how easy it is to deliver these licks, yet I bet your foot will feel the groove. Try to play expressively and listen to the tonal changes from picking within any lick. They sing, even when played so basically.

CHAPTER VI:
The 1980s

Lil' Ed Williams (1955–)

The Chicago-born boogie blues exemplar is the nephew, protégé, and musical heir of J.B. Hutto. In 1975, he formed the first incarnation of the Blues Imperials with his half-brother, bassist James "Pookie" Young. As opposed to many blues musicians who move around, Williams has only led his own band or recorded solo for his entire career. In 1987, Alligator Records included one of Lil' Ed's Blues Imperials tracks on *New Bluebloods* and followed up by releasing their first album, *Roughhousin'*. Famously recorded "live" in one night, the spontaneity and stomping, unvarnished blues would set the template for all the powerful music to come. Two more were issued by Alligator, but after the last, *What You See Is What You Get*, in 1992, Williams broke up the Blues Imperials and went his own way with *Keep on Walkin'* (1996) and *Who's Been Talking* (1998). Williams reunited the band in 1999 for *Get Wild!*, *Heads Up!* (2002), *Rattleshake* (2006), *Full Tilt* (2008), and *Jump Start* (2012). Lil' Ed & the Blues Imperials won the *Blues Music Award* for "Band of the Year" in 2007 and 2009.

Fig. 27: One verse of a Lil' Ed-style shuffle. Simple playing and Ed's enthusiasm come through. He has so much fun playing that it makes us smile to hear it.

Blues Archaeology Williams carries on a blues tradition going back to Son House and continuing up through his uncle J.B. Hutto and Hound Dog Taylor, among others. Essentially, it is to allow the brawny sound of over-amped slide guitar to make the musical statement as opposed to virtuoso technique.

Bernard Allison (1965–)

Bernard is the fiery son of the late virtuoso Chicago blues guitarist Luther Allison, and like him, has lived extensively in Paris though born in the Windy City. He was not only influenced by his father but, when in Koko Taylor's band following high school graduation, also by Johnny Winter on slide guitar and Stevie Ray Vaughan. He formed his first band, Bernard Allison and Back Talk, in 1985, and in 1989, became his father's touring band leader in Europe. That same year, he recorded *The Next Generation* (Teldec Recording Service) with the band and Luther's guidance, and would go on to co-write and arrange songs for his father's last three albums. Three more albums would be released in Europe until 1997, the year Luther died, when *Keepin' the Blues Alive* was released in the US on Ron Levy's Cannonball Records label. Now established at home as a rising young star with talent and charisma, tours and more recordings followed, including *Storms of Life* (#5 Top Blues Album in 2002). His 14th album of power blues and blues rock, *Let It Go*, came out in 2018 on Ruf Records.

Fig. 28: One verse in the style of Bernard Allison. He will play a verse like this solo to introduce a song. Live, the power in his slide playing is Chicago blues slide guitar with a rock feel. I play it twice: first fast and hopefully dazzling; then slower, to hear and see the actual licks.

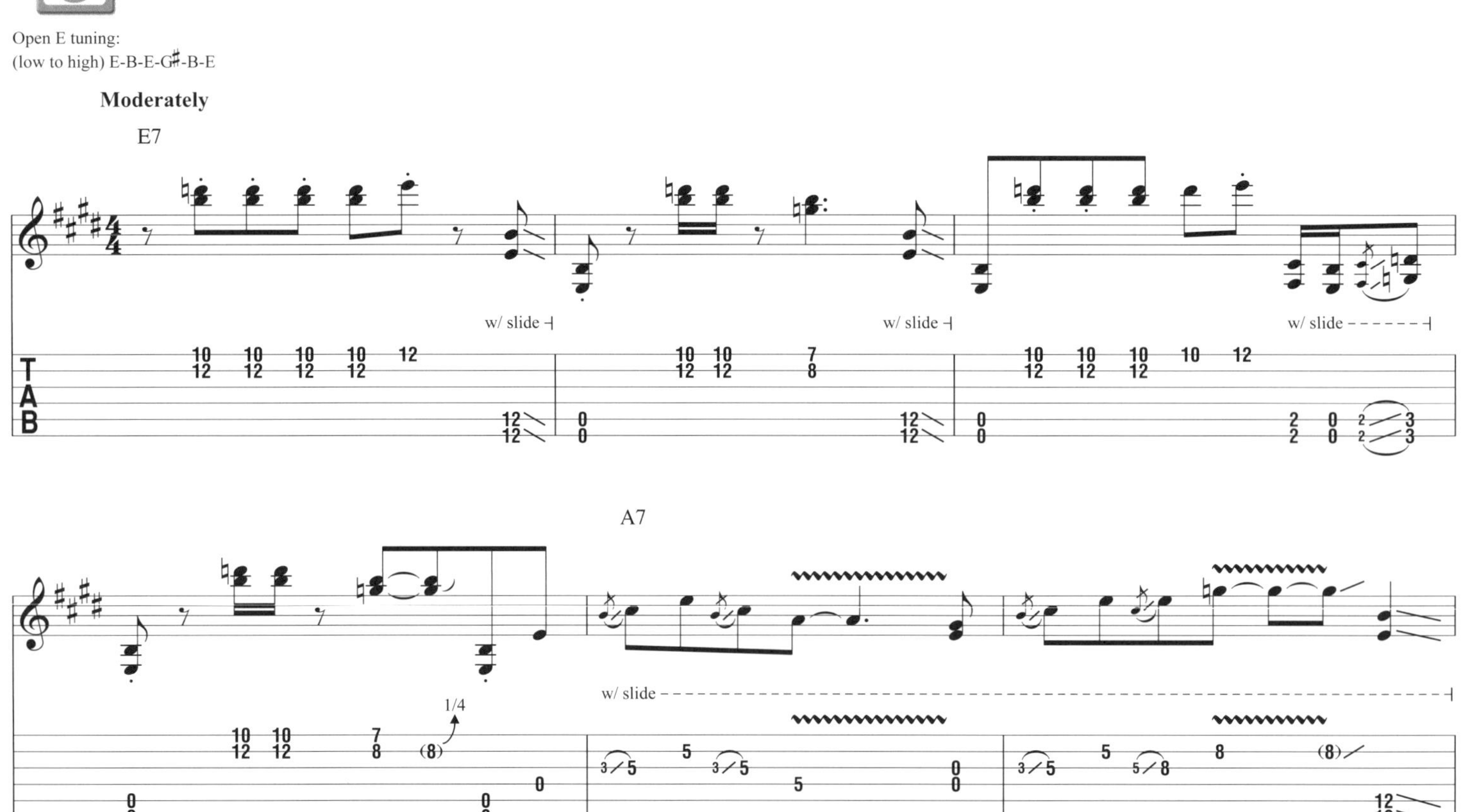

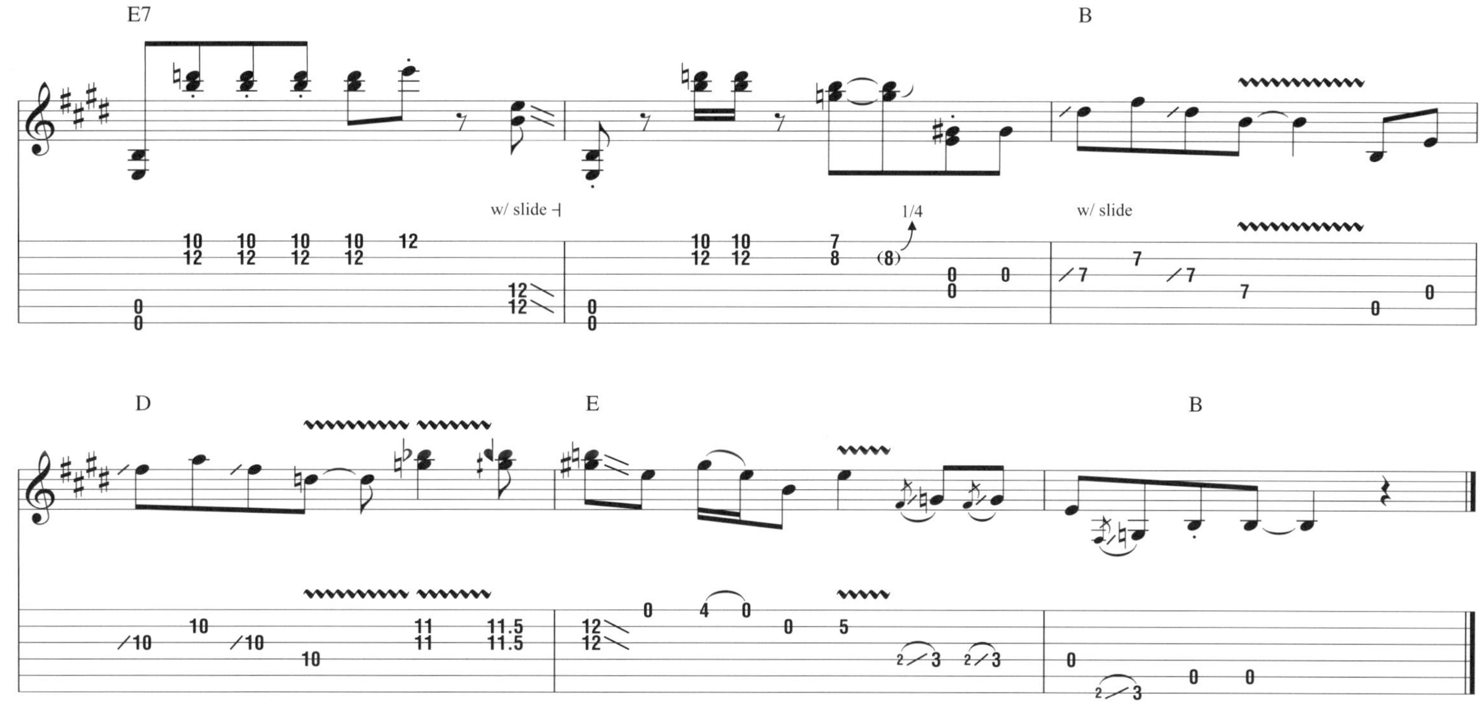

Blues Archaeology **If "turnabout is fair play," then the influence rock guitarists had on young blues guitarists in the latter part of the 20th century attempts at payback for the enormous debt owed the blues originators.**

Studebaker John (1952–)

Hard blues-rocking John "Studebaker John" Grimaldi was born in Chicago like some other young players known for their affinity to the style, and particularly that which had its genesis on the West Side. Even more to the point, his father was an amateur musician and Grimaldi would become a regular denizen on Maxwell Street where he saw Little Walter and Sonny Boy Williamson II, inspiring him to play harp. Experiencing Hound Dog Taylor tearing it up convinced him to learn the guitar, including slide. In the 1970s, he formed a blues-rock band called the Hawks, as the name relates to his classic 1950s Studebaker car. He produced his debut recording, *Straight No Chaser* (Retread Records) in 1979 and has since released 17 more for Blind Pig, Avanti, and Delmark Records. In 1991, he recorded classic Chicago blues with the New Yardbirds and the Pretty Things, while *Songs for None* (2017) finds him playing solo guitar and harp.

Fig. 29: One verse of a shuffle in open E in the style of Studebaker John. John often presents both call and response in his playing, answering his own licks with simple fills that sound good.

Blues Archaeology One of the pertinent advantages of open E or D is the ability to play "cut boogie" patterns on the bottom two bass strings. The open strings provide the I chord harmony, while barring at frets 5 and 7 accesses the IV and V chords, respectively.

Billy Flynn (1956–)

Billy Flynn is one of the most authentic and knowledgeable contemporary Chicago blues guitarists who also claims a background in 1950s and '60s instrumental rock 'n' roll. He has been the versatile, go-to guitarist in Chicago since the mid-1970s when he backed Sunnyland Slim and also began an extended stint with Jimmy Dawkins. Starting in the '80s, he played with local blues bands as well as the Legendary Blues Band and Mississippi Heat. His other credits include Bryan Lee, Little Smokey Smothers, Mark Hummel, Willie Kent, Snooky Pryor, Big Bill Morganfield, John Brim, Jody Williams, Little Arthur Duncan, Deitra Farr, and Billy Boy Arnold. He has released four solo albums starting in 2005 with *Billy's Blues* and *Chicago Blues Mandolin*, followed by *Blues Drive Vol. 1-2* (2009) and *Lonesome Highway* (2017). In 2008, Flynn contributed significant guitar to the Chess Records biopic *Cadillac Records*. In addition, he has been a regular member of the popular traditional Chicago blues band, the Cash Box Kings, most recently adding his stellar guitar to *Royal Mint* (2017).

Fig. 30: A slow blues intro in the style of Billy Flynn. Notice how moving the slide only one fret up or down for the next note can make bluesy playing melodic and evoke older styles of blues.

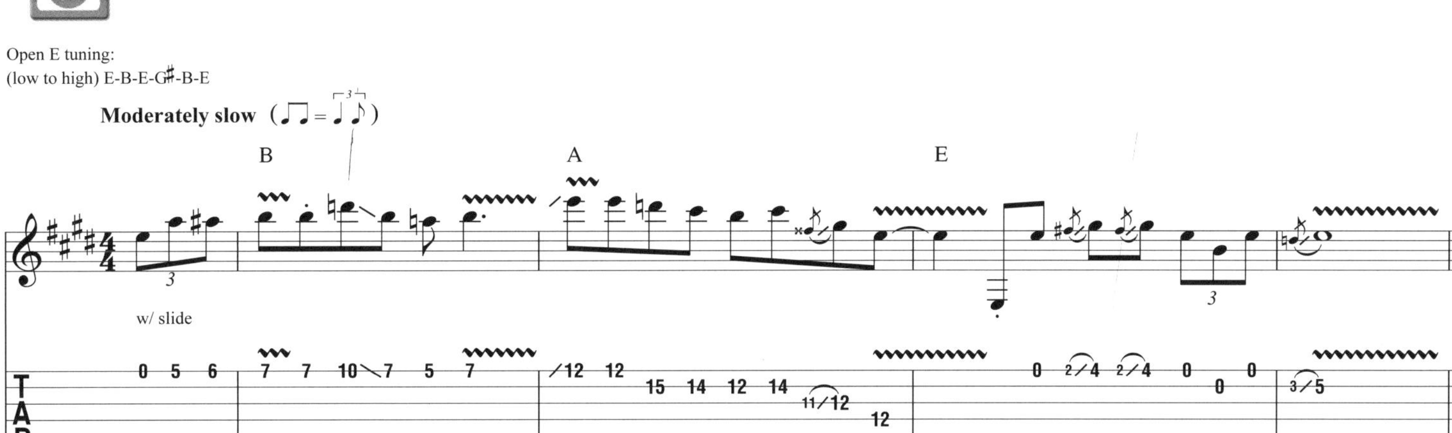

Blues Archaeology A line could be drawn from Robert Nighthawk and Earl Hooker forward to Billy Flynn as regards the expressive playing of slide in standard tuning.

CHAPTER VII:
Muddy Waters' Slide Guitar Style

by Bob Margolin

Muddy Waters' slide guitar style evolved from the acoustic Delta blues he played in the late 1930s through the mid-1940s to the electric Chicago blues he pioneered in the late 1940s, and for the rest of his life. Here's everything I can tell and show you about his slide playing…

Muddy Waters Sparks the Golden Age of Chicago Blues

McKinley "Muddy Waters" Morganfield (1915–1983) moved from Mississippi to Chicago in 1943. He was already a very accomplished Delta blues singer and acoustic slide guitarist and had recorded for the Library of Congress in 1941 and 1942. These recordings demonstrate the roots of Muddy's electric slide playing. They are in open G tuning and show a powerful, deliberate, straightforward slide guitar style which works well in a small combo or solo. In 1971, before I knew Muddy, I went to one of his shows and saw him tune to open G and play this way as the band brought their volume down and simplified their accompaniment. I was in the audience, sitting five feet in front of Muddy. I've never seen or been part of a deeper musical performance. I think it's as close as I could come, given that Muddy was 33 years older than me, to having seen him in the early 1940s in Mississippi.

From here, I'll relate what Muddy himself and his friend and musical partner, Jimmy Rogers, told me about Muddy's early days in Chicago before I was born. I've never written this down before, but it came from the mouths of these thoughtful, self-aware guitar geniuses to my ears decades later. Muddy's stories were related to me when I was in his band in the 1970s, and Jimmy's essential stories were told in 1990, seven years after Muddy passed. Their versions do not contradict written history and biographers, but I'll tell you that what they told me directly is the next best thing to hearing it from their mouths yourself. And I'll tell you what I observed and participated in directly with Muddy from 1973–1980.

Muddy was 28 and Jimmy was 18 when they met and played at Chicago house parties and clubs. They began to use electric guitars with the small amps available in the 1940s. Jimmy told me he taught Muddy to play in standard tuning, and it's telling that Muddy played non-slide, standard-tuning blues on mid-1940s recordings that sunk, unappreciated. But Muddy recorded "Can't Be Satisfied" for Aristocrat Records (precursor of Chess) in 1948. He played Mississippi Delta style in open G tuning but on an electric guitar. He told me it was a Gretsch archtop with an add-on DeArmond pickup played through a small amp cranked enough to sweetly distort, adding singing tone and sustain. Muddy's bold, aggressive slide guitar was accompanied by only percussive upright bass. When the song was released in 1949, it was an instant hit, and Muddy, at the age of 34, became what he called "a known person." He drove through Chicago and heard his song played on jukeboxes and through open windows. "Can't Be Satisfied" gratified Muddy.

That was just the start of why Muddy is an icon of American music. It's my opinion that using a small amp-distorted electric guitar was bold and aggressive. It had the down-home feeling of Delta blues but with a new and then-modern electric sound. With Muddy's great singing, undeniable charisma, and powerful sexuality coming through on his recordings, he became a legend who still inspires young musicians and music lovers 70 years after his first hits.

The success of "Can't Be Satisfied" inspired demand for similar recordings of his electric, minimally backed Delta sound. Though the flip side of that 78 RPM single was "Feel Like Goin' Home," a slower blues in the same style, my favorite from that time is his version of "Walking Blues." Its groove both walks and floats, and Muddy's singing and playing on it are ultimate. Still, both Muddy and Jimmy told me separately this was frustrating because Muddy had a fine small band going with Jimmy on guitar, harp genius Little Walter, and a drummer. Chess Records still went with more hits in the duo or trio format, with no drums. Most were played by Muddy in open G, but he played the classic "Rolling Stone" solo on electric guitar in standard tuning without slide (I won't mention the band who took their name from this song). "Long Distance Call" with upright bass had Muddy playing slide in standard tuning and Little Walter's supportive acoustic harp before he was allowed to use an amplifier. The guitar and harp were "filling in the cracks," to use a Jimmy Rogers expression for what they called their deliberately interweaving arrangements. Jimmy Rogers himself was not on this recording, but soon...

Muddy convinced Chess to record his whole band, and by 1951, they added piano master Otis Spann. This began what is sometimes known as the "Golden Age" of electric Chicago blues. The signature interplay of their arrangements was both natural and intended. Jimmy Rogers told me that sometimes after gigs, the band—unofficially known as the Headcutters—would ride around the streets of Chicago planning musical magic for the bandstand to compete with the other fine bluesmen getting popular then, like Howlin' Wolf, Elmore James, and Jimmy Reed. They would do guest sets in clubs that were so powerful they would get hired. They also toured, fueled by their hits that reached beyond Chicago. Muddy's electric slide was always a showstopper, even with geniuses like Otis Spann, Little Walter, and Jimmy Rogers featured.

In the late 1950s and early '60s, Muddy continued to record regularly for Chess but the Golden Age of Chicago Blues was over. Still, some of Muddy's greatest albums and compilations were released: *The Best of Muddy Waters* (1958) and *Live at Newport* (1960). *Muddy Waters Folk Singer* (1964) tried to cash in on the popular folk music trend, but turned out to be a spectacular acoustic blues album with Willie Dixon on upright bass and a young Buddy Guy on guitar. There was also an excellent double album compilation, *McKinley Morganfield: A.K.A. Muddy Waters*. I still know every crackle and pop on my vinyl copy.

Chess was definitely trying to market Muddy to the young blues audience created by the British and American bands who idolized his music. Two controversial albums were released around 1970, *Electric Mud* and *After the Rain*. Producer Marshall Chess, Chess Records, and some fans purported that the albums were groundbreaking. Muddy's dedicated blues audience, who loved him for being raw and real, were disappointed. For what it's worth, those albums didn't work for me, but I'm very open to blues and rock music combined. More importantly, I asked Muddy about them only a few years later, and he just hung his head and shook it "no," slowly.

By the time I joined Muddy's band in 1973, he was playing music clubs and concerts worldwide, from Carnegie Hall and an Allman Brothers tour to small bars. Muddy was 58 and called "The Old Man" by his band. His final album for Chess Records was *The Woodstock Album* (1975), produced by Levon Helm from the Band, Paul Butterfield, and Henry Glover.

Levon brought Muddy, with me and Pinetop Perkins, to *The Last Waltz* concert in 1976. The Martin Scorsese film of the concert is still the most visible moment of Muddy's career, and mine too, as I was standing right next to him. I always wished that Muddy had played some classic slide guitar on it, but "Mannish Boy" certainly was strong. Just before *The Last Waltz* concert, Muddy left Chess Records. He explained to me, "Chess Records was sold to a corporation and there was nobody from the Chess family still involved."

In October of 1976, a month before *The Last Waltz*, Muddy recorded *Hard Again*, produced by Johnny Winter for his new Blue Sky label. It definitely sparked a big jump in Muddy's visibility, though he played no guitar at all on it. At his shows, however, Muddy *always* still showcased his slide guitar playing to standing ovations. The next two albums for Blue Sky, *I'm Ready* and *Muddy "Mississippi" Waters Live*, had plenty of Muddy's fully matured slide guitar playing in slow blues songs. As he said, "Slow blues is where the soul is. I'd play nothing but that if I could."

Numerous videos of Muddy playing slide during that era exist, including some from European shows that were professionally filmed. I co-produced reissues of Muddy's four Blue Sky albums, and I used my experience as one of the musicians and as a producer to keep the new recordings true to the original performances. I recommend the *Muddy "Mississippi" Waters Live Legacy Edition*, which took the original album and added a CD of previously unheard recordings of Muddy in a club with his own band. In 2008, I produced *Breakin' It Up, Breakin' It Down*, which contains live, previously unreleased recordings of Muddy from a 1977 tour with Johnny Winter and James Cotton, supporting *Hard Again*.

By the end of the 1970s, Muddy's health began to decline, and he missed some gigs. It got slowly worse over the next few years as he had heart disease and lung cancer, though he had quit smoking in 1973. In 1983, I phoned Muddy on his birthday, April 4. I asked him if, now that he was off the road due to illness, he ever picked up his guitar just to play it. He replied, "Naw, I've been playing 50 years, it's there." Somehow, my last words to him on that phone call were "Be strong." It broke my heart that he was "going down slow." He soon passed at home on April 30, 1983, but his music is more popular than ever. He would be gratified and satisfied to know that *you* are interested in learning about his style of slide guitar playing. Whether you try to copy it exactly, or just take inspiration, Muddy will live again in your music.

Muddy Waters' Slide Guitar Techniques

In the 1940s, Chicago blues slide guitarists began to use electric guitars, be they acoustic archtop or flattop with add-on pickups, or guitars with built-in pickups. Solid body guitars were just a few years in the future. It really was Muddy Waters who broke through and stood out from the others in the Chicago blues genre, starting with his 1949 hit, "Can't Be Satisfied."

Once, in the 1970s, when Muddy broke a string onstage, he handed me his slide and had me tune up to open A. I played "Walking Blues" while he sang it. When it came time for me to take the guitar solo, he commanded, "Make it ring!" He grunted when I did my best, and he liked it. Muddy the guitar player loved the power of "Chicago Blues Slide Guitar" and wanted to use me to deliver it while his own guitar was down. I used the same heavy strings as he did, and even with lower action than the almost unplayable high action Mud used, on my guitar, the sustained slide notes with vibrato did indeed ring.

The key to Muddy's picking-hand approach to slide guitar is that he played electric guitar with the same forceful touch as he had played acoustic slide in Mississippi. Then, he was going for volume as well as musical power. He had to play an unamplified guitar loud enough to be heard solo or with other musicians in a juke joint with people partying and dancing. He used pure physical force with his picking hand. This is a large part of why Muddy sounds like Muddy on any guitar: acoustic, archtop with add-on pickup, an early trapeze-bridge Les Paul Goldtop, or his signature 1957 Telecaster. He is seen in rare photos with other guitars, but those were his main ones. In the late 1960s, Muddy used a Guild guitar when the company endorsed his band. Whatever guitar we use, if we want to sound like Muddy, we need to play aggressively, not tentatively.

Originally white with a maple neck, Muddy told me he had the 1957 Telecaster painted red and replaced the neck with a rosewood neck in 1961, as Fender offered a wider neck option in the 1960s. I remember seeing that in Fender catalogs in 1965, and Muddy went for it because he had big hands. I used to take care of that guitar when I was in his band. Muddy told me all those details when I asked, and for a player who was a force of nature, he also understood electric guitars and amps and how they worked together.

In a recently discovered 1981 video interview, Muddy said "I have my old Fender; I believe it's a '56…" Maybe he acquired the '56 in '57, or maybe he told me wrong in the 1970s when he said "'57." Either way, it's one of the most important electric guitars in music history. It's often been displayed in museum exhibits, including at the Metropolitan Museum of Art in New York City in 2019. Muddy also said he started using amplifiers to be heard in noisy clubs and taverns. But note that he also recorded with electric guitars. Before he got the love-of-his-life Telecaster, he had a Gretsch archtop with a DeArmond pickup, followed by an early Les Paul Goldtop with a trapeze tailpiece.

On the following pages are examples of Muddy's slide playing style that made them crave the sound of an electric guitar with a small amp cranked enough to enhance the tone: An electric sound that was bold and cutting edge.

Fig. 31: Muddy mused, "My music is so simple to play..." Good for us, we can find the notes easily. Then Muddy wondered, "but so few can play it right." That means we have to find an expressive and percussive touch to put blues into these simple notes with a slide and our fingers.

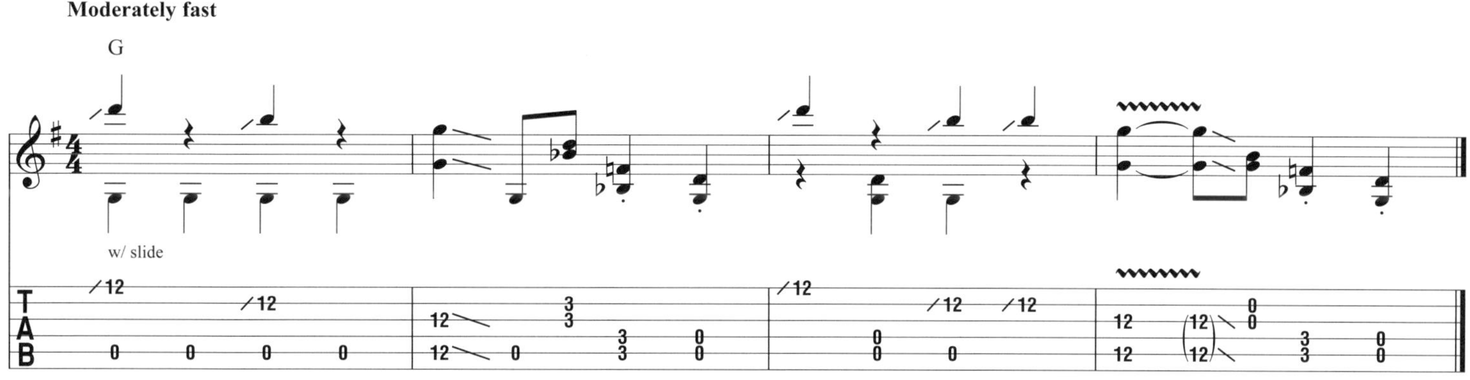

Blues Archaeology B.B. King once said something similar with, "The blues is simple music. Anyone can play it. But would you want to hear anyone play it?" The same could be said for the monumental blues of Muddy Waters.

Fig. 32: Another classic, fast, open G song that came from Delta blues before Muddy brought it to Chicago. This one has the melody on string 1, then a rhythm lick on the middle strings to fill in. This is hard to play with a flat pick because it requires thumb and fingers and palm-on-bridge, damped picking (palm muting) to make it snappy. I've slowed it down here.

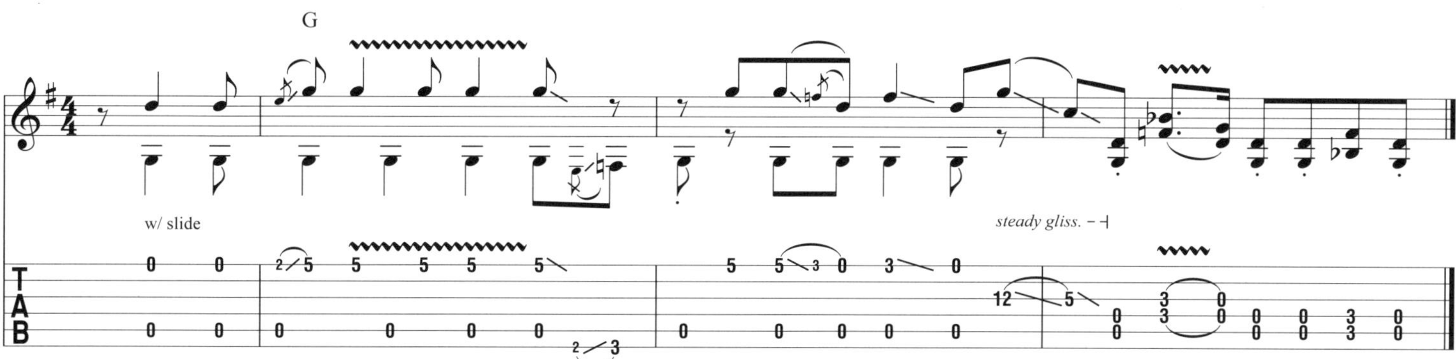

Fig. 33: More open G. Here is the melody lick on the open high string, while the cool, distinctive lick falls with the slide on the lower strings at fret 3.

Open G tuning:
(low to high) D-G-D-G-B-D

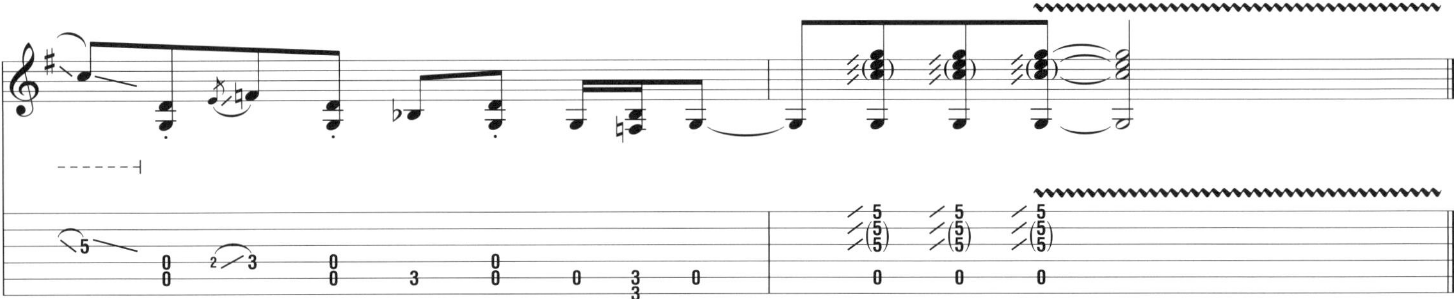

Blues Archaeology **The chord at fret 3 in open G tuning is B♭, the "nasty" ♭III. The root of the chord is also the gritty ♭3rd "blues note" (not a "*blue* note") from the blues scale, and one of the defining notes of the blues.**

Fig. 34: Muddy's turnarounds in open G tuning often had just single-string lines on string 5 up to fret 7 for the V chord, and back down to fret 5 for the IV chord. They are simple, clear, and bluesy.

Open G tuning:
(low to high) D-G-D-G-B-D

Blues Archaeology **A great example of "less is more"—an approach and attitude found more often in prewar acoustic blues than postwar electric blues.**

A single-string turnaround is a classic Muddy-style lick. In late 1978, Muddy began a European tour opening for Eric Clapton. Muddy didn't know who Eric was. At breakfast with Mud on the third day of the tour, I told him Eric was deeply influenced by Robert Johnson, as he was. I suggested Muddy stay for Eric's set rather than going back to the hotel immediately after his opening set. Muddy did. In the middle of his set, Eric played "Come See Me Early in the Morning" in open G with a slide. Muddy smiled through Eric's solo, but when Eric played this turnaround, Muddy jumped up and smiled, "That *my* shit!" They became close friends that night, bonding over the turnaround.

Fig. 35: Here is a simple version of Muddy's slow blues, open G turnaround that both he and Eric played.

Open G tuning:
(low to high) D-G-D-G-B-D

Moderately slow

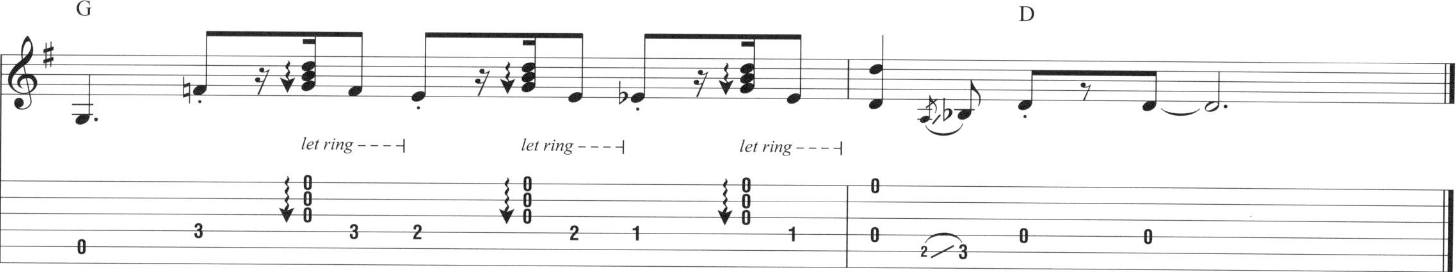

Blues Archaeology **Clapton can be heard playing Muddy's turnaround on the *Unplugged* version of "Walking Blues."**

Open G minor tuning is a murky Muddy mystery to me. In 1994, 11 years after Muddy passed, Chess Records released some live Swiss radio sessions. They were recorded in 1972, before I was in Muddy's band, by a promoter who is my friend now. Muddy played his "Feel Like Going Home" classic slow blues that was on the flip side of his breakthrough song "Can't Be Satisfied." The styles of those 1948 recordings were done in open G tuning as previously mentioned and demonstrated. But for this radio session, Muddy played in open G minor. When I first heard this minor version on the Swiss session, I was stunned, but it was too late to call Muddy and ask him about it.

He played in open G, or A occasionally, when I was in his band. When he did, he often pulled off his picks. I can tell he was playing with no picks on the G minor Swiss recording because he often percussively popped a low string—a trademark of Son House and other Delta blues players from whom Muddy learned. I have used this tuning myself to lend an eerie sound to my slide playing. Before writing about open G minor, I listened with slide guitar master Warren Haynes to Muddy's minor key recording for the first time in about 20 years. My best guess is that Muddy did it deliberately, and since he was almost 60 years old, he had probably done it before. But regardless of Muddy's intention or history, we have a very distinctive, evocative variation of open tuning slide guitar style to consider. If you use that tuning and find your own fingered chords and licks between the slide notes, your audience will feel the sad blues of the song, and blues guitar players will be intrigued and impressed.

Fig. 36: Opening lick in open G minor with a slide up to the IV chord.

Open Gm tuning:
(low to high) D-G-D-G-B♭-D

Slow

Gm

Cm

w/ slide

Blues Archaeology **Minor key slide blues are rare, but minor keys were significant in the non-slide classics of West Side of Chicago legends Otis Rush ("Double Trouble," "All Your Love: I Miss Loving," "My Love Will Never Die") and Magic Sam ("All Your Love," "Easy Baby").**

With his larger bands from the early 1950s on, Muddy most often played in standard tuning. He preferred to play in the keys of E or A with their signature blues chord shapes and scales. Yet he liked to sing in G or A, so he would capo up to those keys but still play in first-position E or A fingerings. With a capo at fret 3, he would be playing in G but fingering the E position, or in C when fingering the A position.

His guitar awaited him onstage with the capo on fret 3. He asked me to tune it *after* the capo was put on, because the capo changed the scale length and he wanted his guitar both in tune with itself and the standard pitch of the band, which included the fixed-pitch piano and harmonica. He called the capo a "clamp." If he moved or removed the clamp, he would retune quickly by ear. He would hit a string he was tuning clearly and tune to just below correct pitch, and then tighten the tuner to raise its pitch until the note was in tune. He told me specifically that the guitar would stay in tune better that way than by tuning down to the note. For the following examples, I'll play without the "clamp." It will be easier for you to see what's happening.

Fig. 37: One verse of solo slide guitar in standard tuning in the style of Muddy Waters. He sometimes added expressive slides or picked in triplets with power, but this is a basic version.

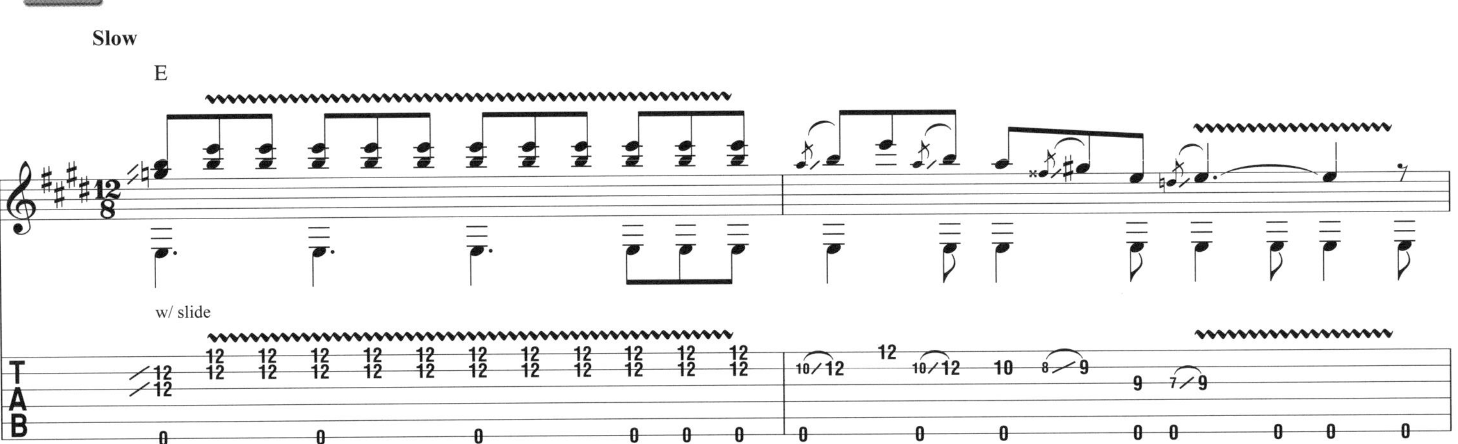

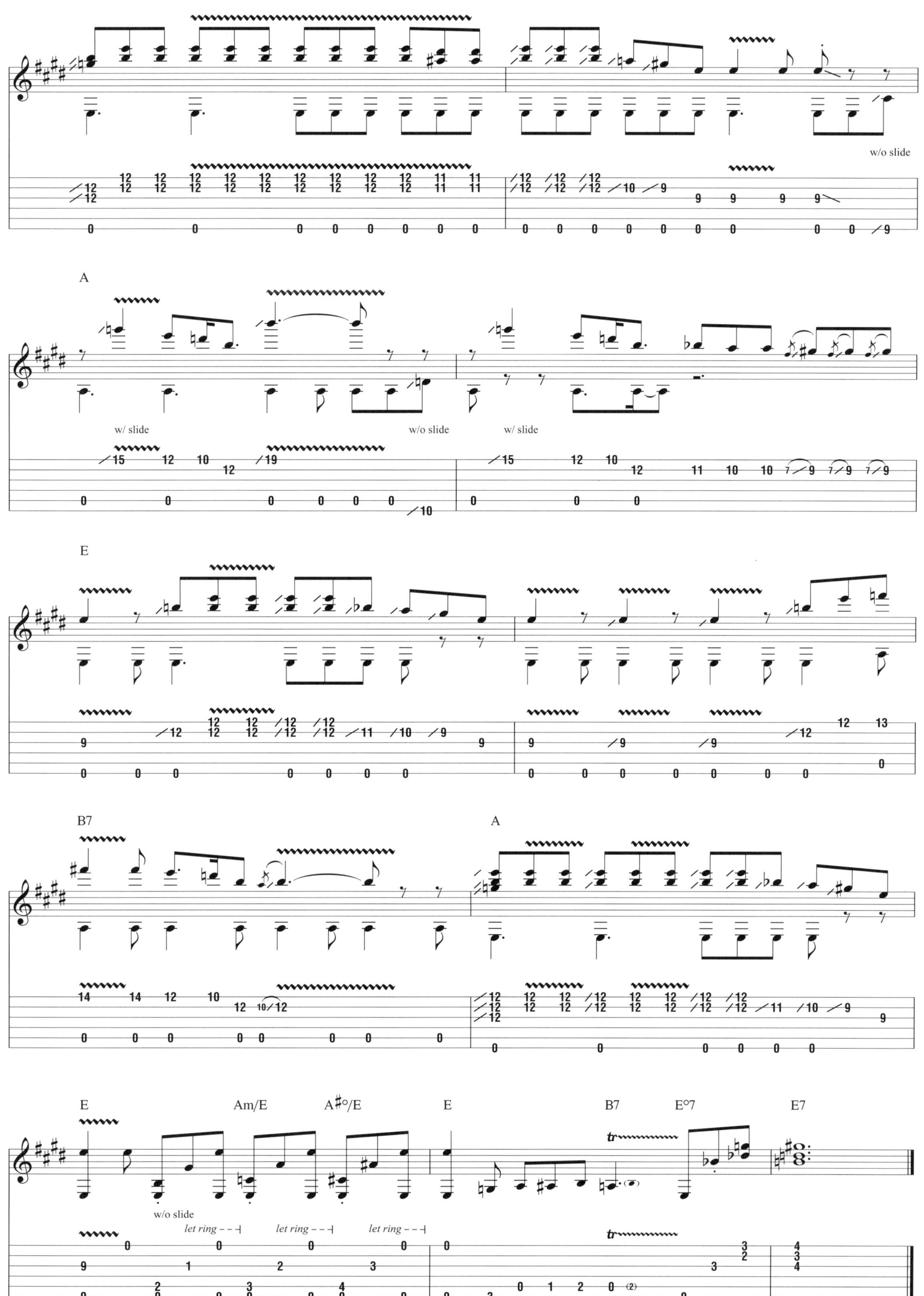
w/o slide
A
w/ slide
w/o slide
w/ slide
E
B7
A
E
Am/E
A♯°/E
E
B7
E°7
E7
w/o slide
let ring
let ring
let ring
tr
tr

Performing live, when Muddy took his slide solos, he would very deliberately solo for two verses. Muddy's standard approach was to make a statement in the first verse, usually using the full-sounding neck pickup of his Telecaster. The intensity of his playing would build at the end of the first verse, and he would switch pickups to the louder, brighter bridge pickup and play the solo's second verse with even more intensity. At the end of that second verse, he would do what he called a "send back" on the last two measures—he would send the focus of the song back to his singing or to the next soloist.

Fig. 38: A classic Muddy turnaround leading into a pickup change from the deep neck pickup to the biting bridge pickup over a hammer-on/pull-off (trill) between B and A on string 5, and into the next solo with the more cutting tone.

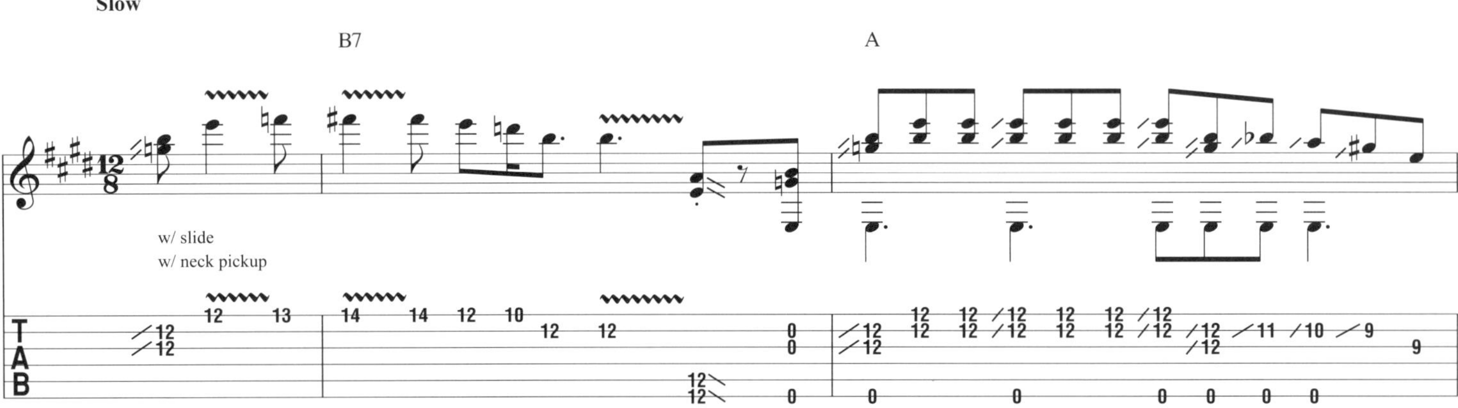

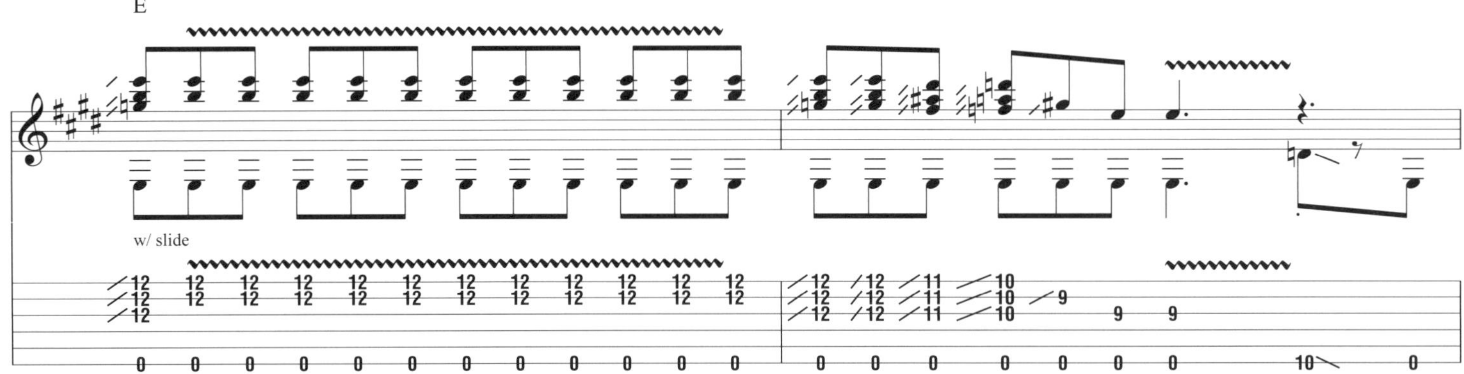

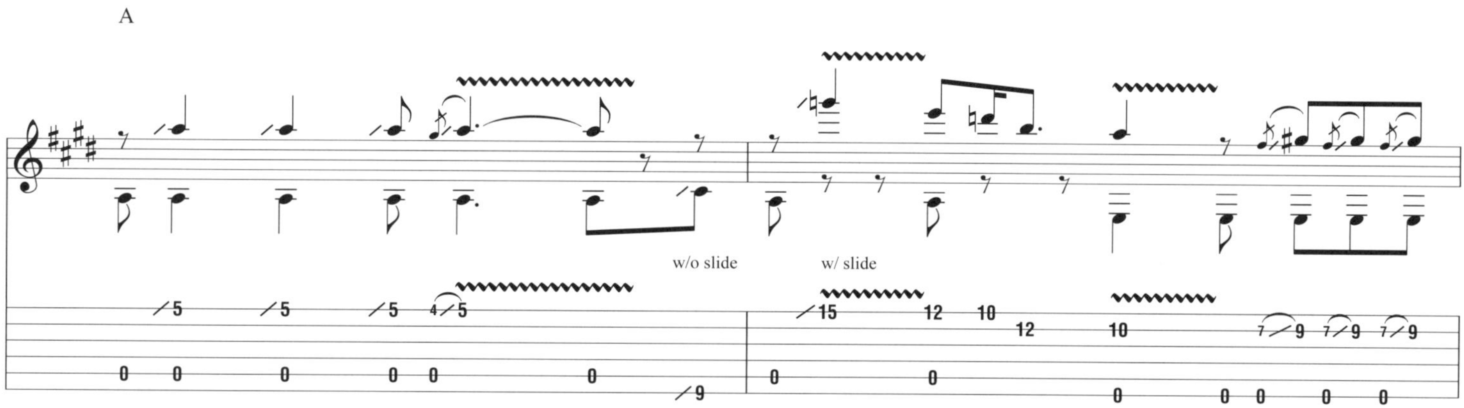

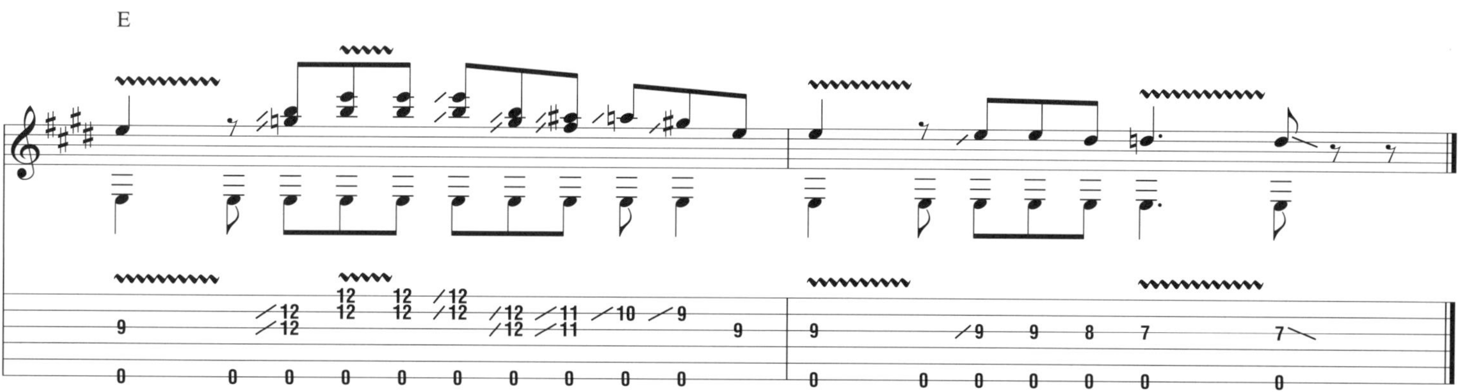

Blues Archaeology Switching from bass to treble tone can be made on virtually any two-pickup (or even three-pickup) guitar, for dynamic effect. However, the difference in register is particularly dramatic on a standard Telecaster—Muddy's axe of choice.

Here are two examples of Muddy's slide playing that go beyond his trademark slow blues soloing…

Fig. 39: In the style of Muddy playing slide licks over a minor key backing, in the key of C minor.

Blues Archaeology Playing several slide notes in a row on one string is a Muddy Waters characteristic contributing to the "vocal" nature of his soloing.

Fig. 40: Muddy-style slide on a jump groove in standard tuning in E. The E lick, when slid like this, is actually an E6, with the slide over fret 9.

Blues Archaeology **One of the challenges when playing slide in standard tuning is finding easily accessible chord forms. One of the best methods is to take open strings 4, 3, and 2 (G major) and move them up the fingerboard with the slide as a small barre. Hence, E (I) is over fret 9, A (IV) over fret 14, and B (V) over fret 16 (or fret 4, an octave below).**

Permit me to ask a question about Muddy's slide playing that I've never heard asked before. I didn't challenge Muddy with it when I played with him because, though it occurred to me, Muddy's slide playing felt so good that the question just stayed in the back of my unused mind while I listened to him with my heart. On slow blues after slow blues, live and recorded, why did Muddy play damn near the same slide solo? It was never *exactly* the same, but it was close in construction. Sometimes he'd play it sparsely, or sometimes he'd spice it up by picking triplets or sliding to a high note for a second, but it was essentially the same solo.

It's certainly not for a lack of creativity, and we must remember that his vocals and the backing musicians on a particular song had a lot to do with why one song sounded different from another. Whether Muddy deliberately chose not to improvise or to craft a unique slide solo on every song, that's just how Muddy played slide.

CHAPTER VIII:
Johnny Winter

Texan Johnny Winter became a rock star and guitar hero in the late 1960s. His first two albums debuted his powerful, loud, and fast-fingered signature take on blues. In 1976, Johnny used his fame to produce collaborations with Muddy Waters: *Hard Again, I'm Ready, Muddy "Mississippi" Waters Live*, and *King Bee*. When he played slide guitar with Muddy live and on recordings, how can we not consider him a "Chicago Blues Slide Guitar" player?

I backed up Johnny and Muddy on those albums and live shows, and also became friends with Johnny. He passed in 2014, but those years he worked with Muddy inspired him to play blues music for the rest of his life—an artistic choice, considering he could have made more money playing to his larger rock audience.

Between the first two Muddy albums in 1977, Johnny recorded the prophetically-titled *Nothin' but the Blues*, fresh from the Hard Again tour with Muddy and with the same musicians who were tight from that tour. Johnny asked me to lead the band behind him on the recording, counting off the songs, cuing the players, and deliberately letting Johnny concentrate on doing his best singing and guitar playing. Many of the songs featured Johnny's slide guitar at a time in his life when he was strongest, physically and musically. Let's consider Johnny Winter's Chicago blues slide guitar style…

Though he recorded in that style from his first albums through his later ones, I'm choosing examples in the style of *Nothin' but the Blues* because I played second guitar on it. He had Chicago blues musicians recording with him, and I know (with the benefit of hindsight) that he was deliberately applying himself to this style at a time when he had more experience than on his first albums, and he was full of inspiration.

Fig. 41: Electric slide blues in open G in the style of Johnny Winter and influenced by Delta blues.

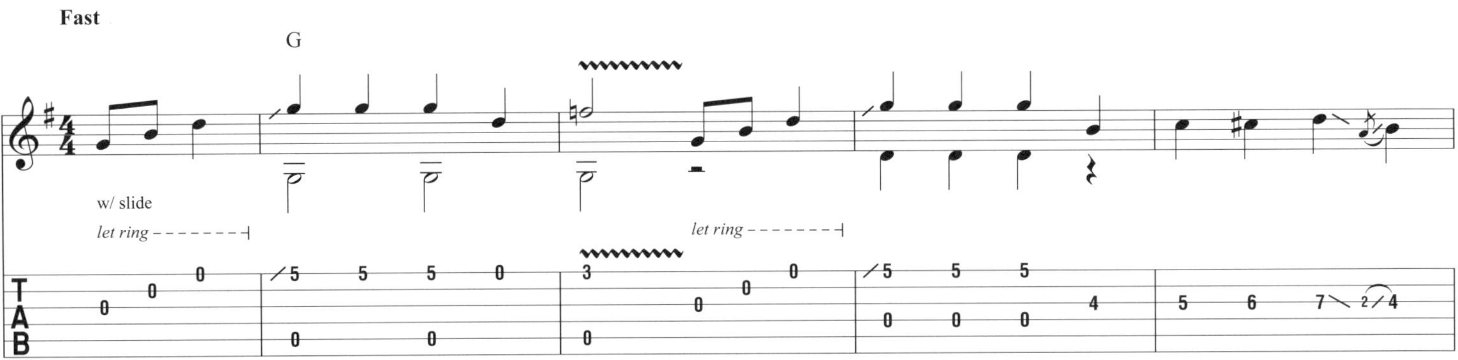

Fig. 42: Slide guitar shuffle in open E in the style of Johnny Winter. Johnny is one of few players who are instantly recognizable.

Open E tuning:
(low to high) E-B-E-G♯-B-E

Moderately

E A E

w/ slide

A

8va

loco

E B

A E

let ring

Blues Archaeology

Blues Archaeology Johnny Winter carried on a particular slide guitar tradition by using homemade slides. However, instead of breaking the neck off a wine bottle, he had one cut from a drummer's hi-hat stand, which was relatively thin and light. He also had one made from pipe bought at a hardware store. Well-known for using a thumb pick rather than a flat pick, he once told an interviewer in the 1970s that after he found a medium Gibson which suited him, he bought up as many as he could find as he was afraid they would not always be available. Later on, he began using Fender medium thumb picks.

CHAPTER IX:
Bob Margolin Master Class

There's a photo of teenage me in my room playing slide guitar—one of the first times I tried. A portable electric typewriter is in the photo, too. The photo is lost but I remember it well, over 50 years later, because I realized that the moment had prophetic personal meaning. Time confirms that playing slide guitar and writing about blues have been big parts of my life. I first heard Chicago blues on a blues radio show. When the DJ played Muddy featuring his slide, I fell in deep and haven't crawled out yet. It felt and sounded right to me, and the depth thrilled me musically. Now I have even more passion for slide guitar, and I have developed my own styles and "signature licks" (a Hal Leonard specialty). I hope they will inspire you.

Let's start with my development of Muddy slide styles that grew from years playing on bandstands and recordings with him. I deliberately avoided trying to reproduce what he played, but I'm grateful for his influence. What I add to my Muddy foundation comes from decades on bandstands since 1980, crafting recordings, combining the techniques inspired by other players, and my own touch and feel.

My technique for the following demonstrated licks and verses is playing with my slide on my fretting-hand pinky, so I can use the rest of the fingers on that hand for chording in both open and standard tunings. And I use a thumb pick with bare fingers to have a wide range of picking styles available to me from moment to moment.

Fig. 43: My version of the classic "Rollin' and Tumblin'" licks as I play them now. On the turnaround, I play slide in octaves, taking advantage of open G tuning, where octaves that line up over one fret can be slid.

Open G tuning:
(low to high) D-G-D-G-B-D

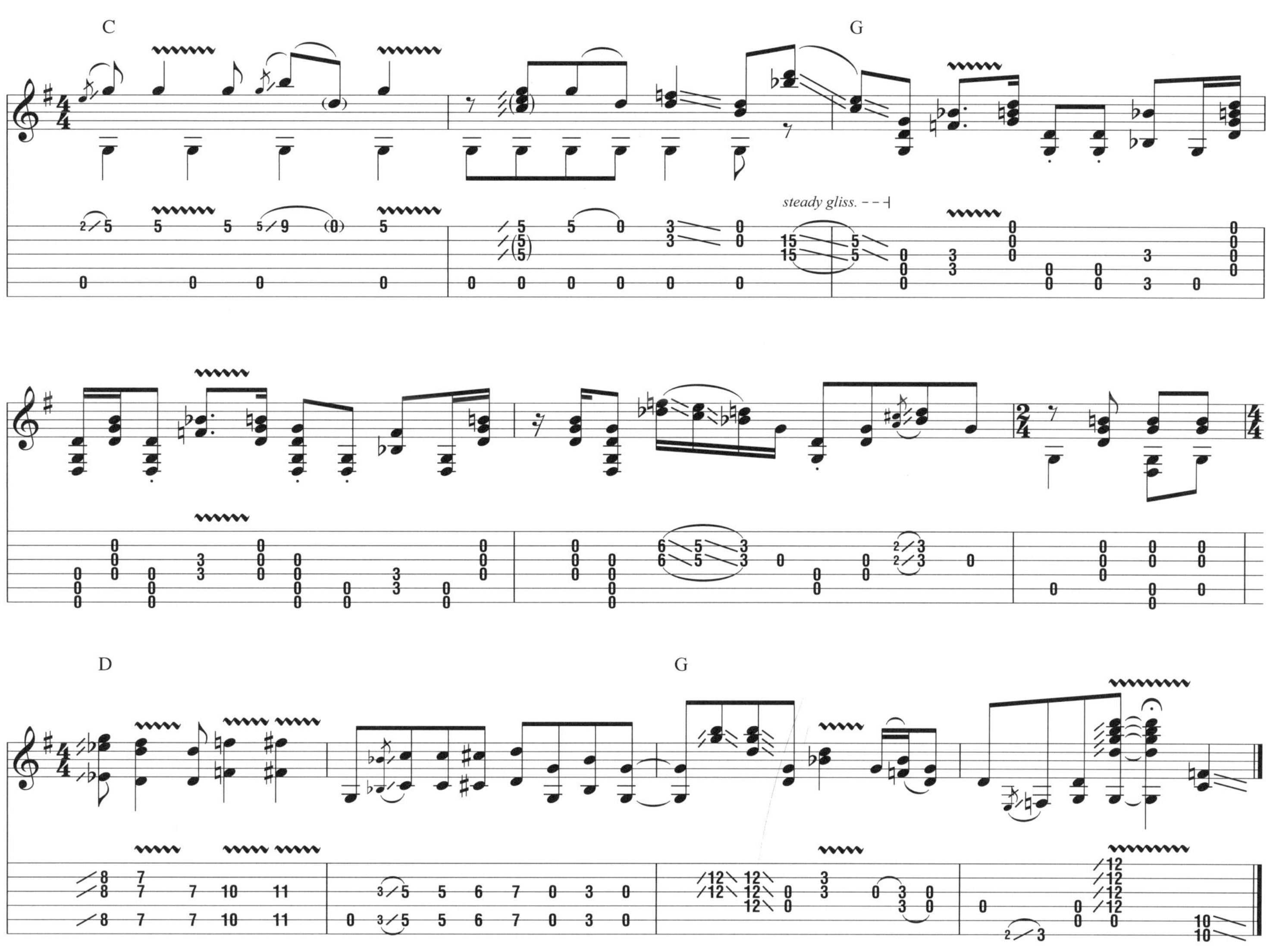

Fig. 44: A Muddy-style slide solo in standard tuning in E, as I play it—interpreting rather than reproducing. I borrow Muddy's classic turnaround from his open G slide but find the notes on different frets in standard tuning. I saw Muddy do this only once in all his solos that I backed or heard, and that was all I needed to learn the lesson. I still do it very occasionally to keep some surprises in my Muddy-style, standard-tuning slide intros or solos. The principle of using open-tuning slide licks in standard tuning makes for an original presentation of traditional licks. We can play the same licks across different tunings by just finding the notes, wherever they may be.

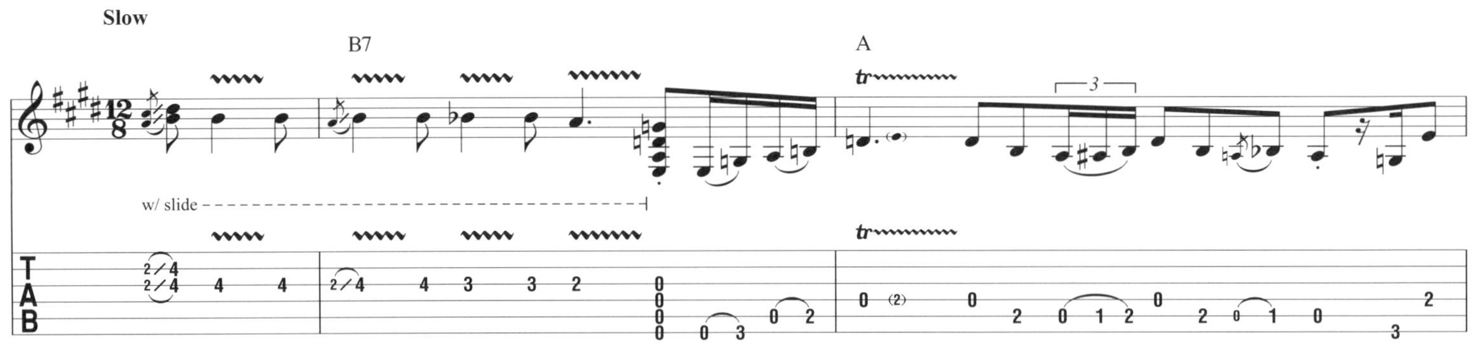
Slow
B7
A
tr
3
w/ slide

E
Am/E
A♯°/E
E7
B7
tr
let ring
let ring
let ring

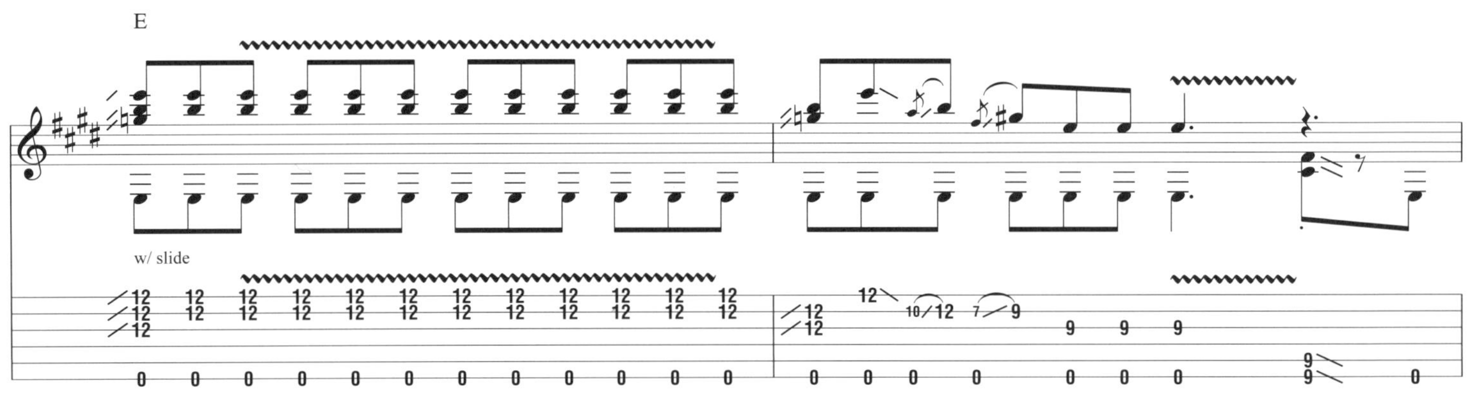
E
w/ slide

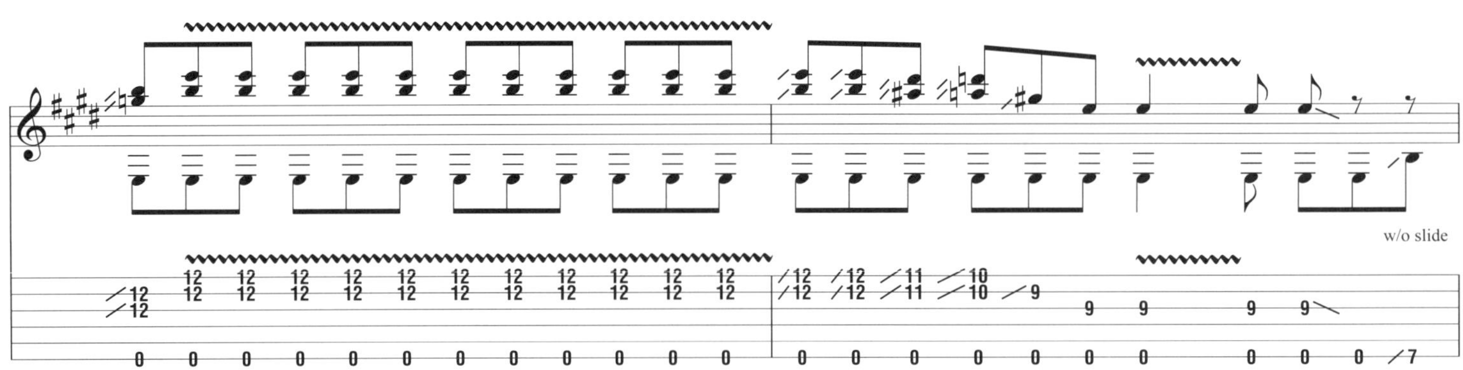
w/o slide

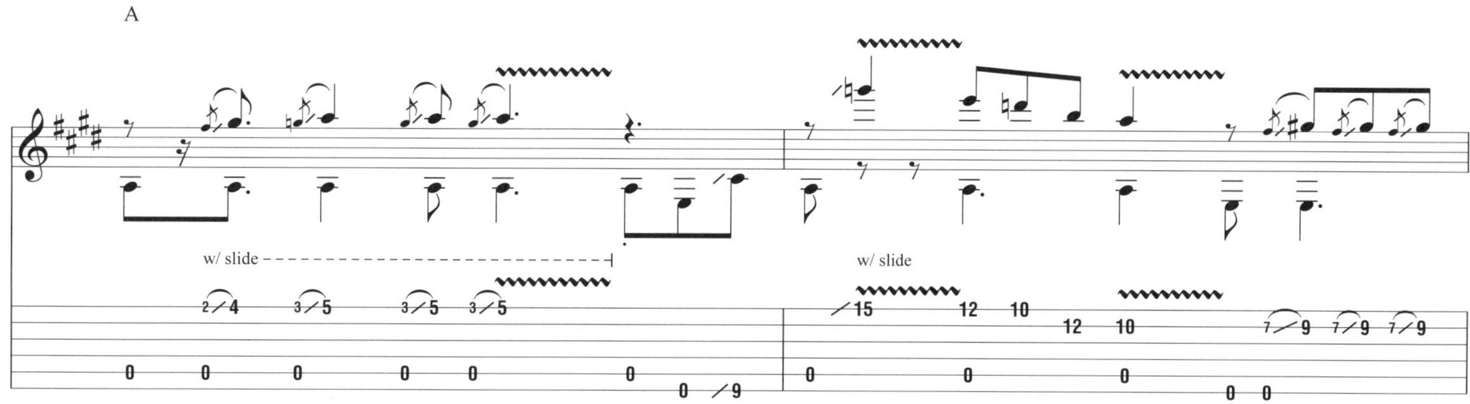

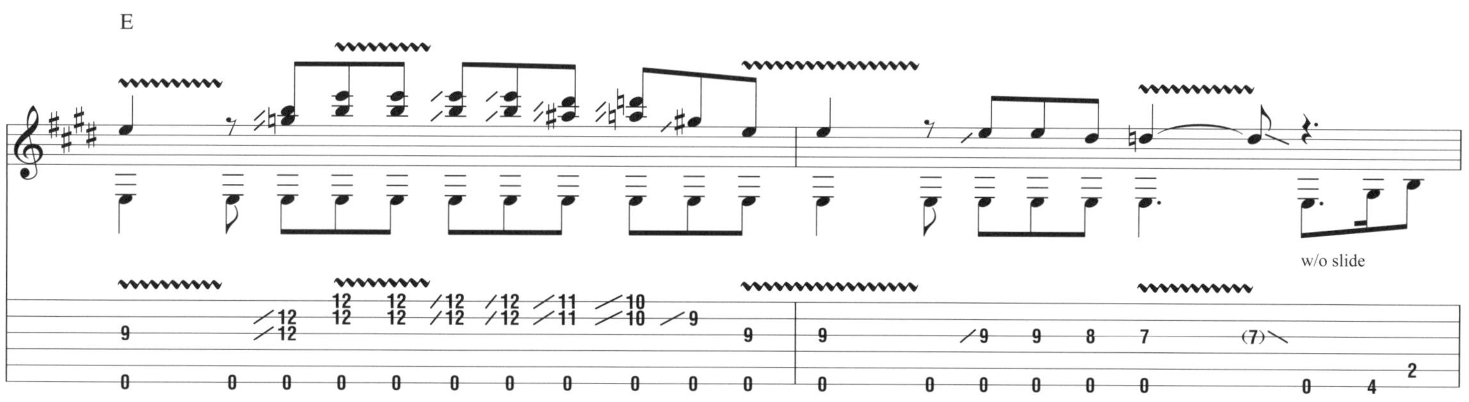

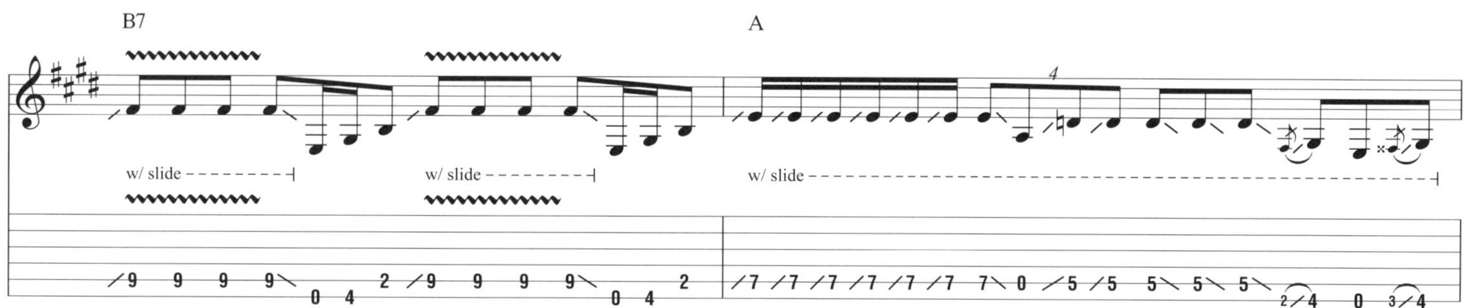

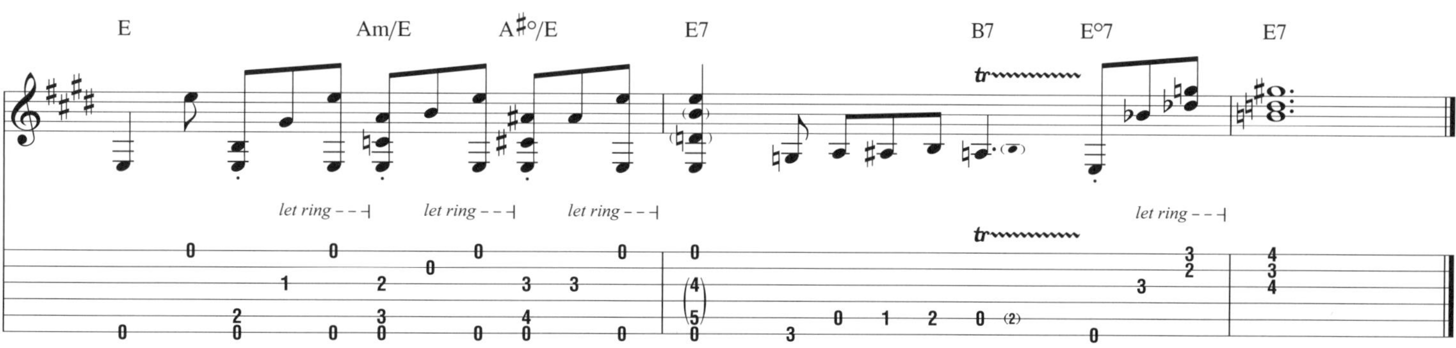

Blues Archaeology The ♭3rd (G) in the key of E, which occurs on string 3 at fret 12 in the octave E blues box, can be a grating tone in the wrong hands. However, Bob takes advantage of the dissonance and makes it roar with blues power.

Fig. 45: I play two verses of a solo here. Notice how the end of the first leads into more intensity in the second without changing the tone of the guitar, but just by playing triplets, digging in, and picking harder. The ghosts of some of my favorite slide players are in this song, a tribute to women who go out to hear blues music. Indeed, one vocal verse begins with "To her, nothing sounds so good as a ringing slide guitar."

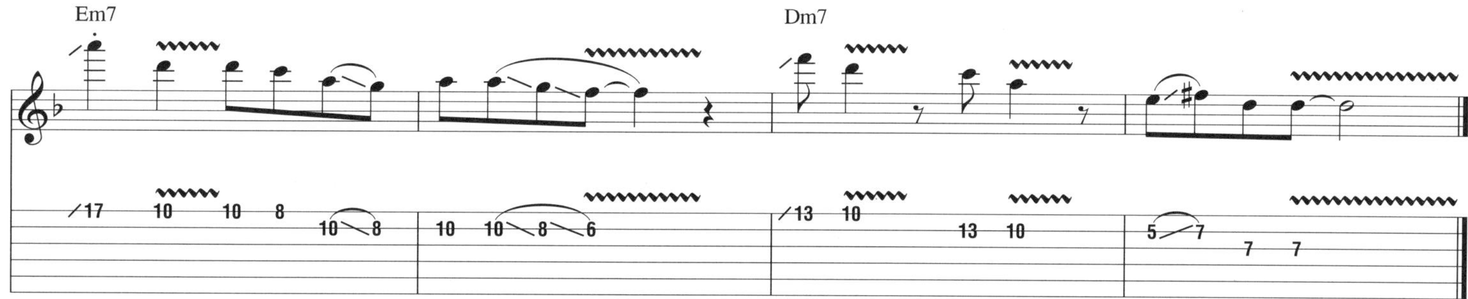

Fig. 46: Chicago blues shuffle with two guitars. One plays thumped low strings and melody chords in A. The slide guitar part is tuned to play conventional open A slides one octave lower, on the lower three strings. I made up this tuning for this one song. Aside from this unique tuning, the point is that you can make the guitar play whatever you want: Find your own way. The guitar is tuned very unconventionally, low to high: A-C♯-E-A-C♯-E.

Tuning:
(low to high) A-C♯-E-A-C♯-E

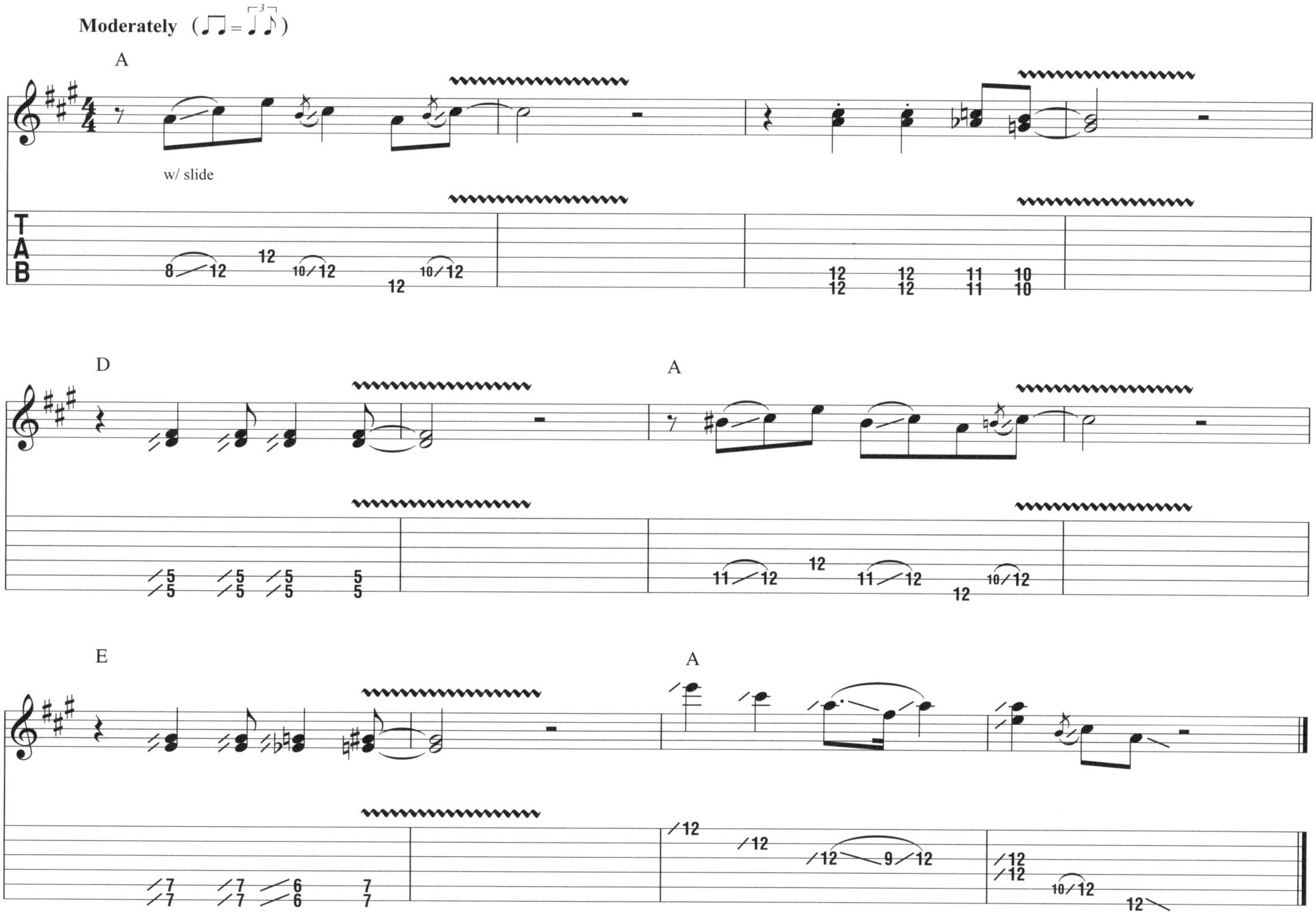

Moderately (♫ = ♩ ♪ triplet)

A

w/ slide

D

A

E

A

Fig. 47: These are open D classic licks re-arranged. When I recorded an open D slide shuffle, I took the opportunity to *not* use standard, open D licks as Elmore James and so many others had done. I used the same scale and phrasing but created different melodies with them.

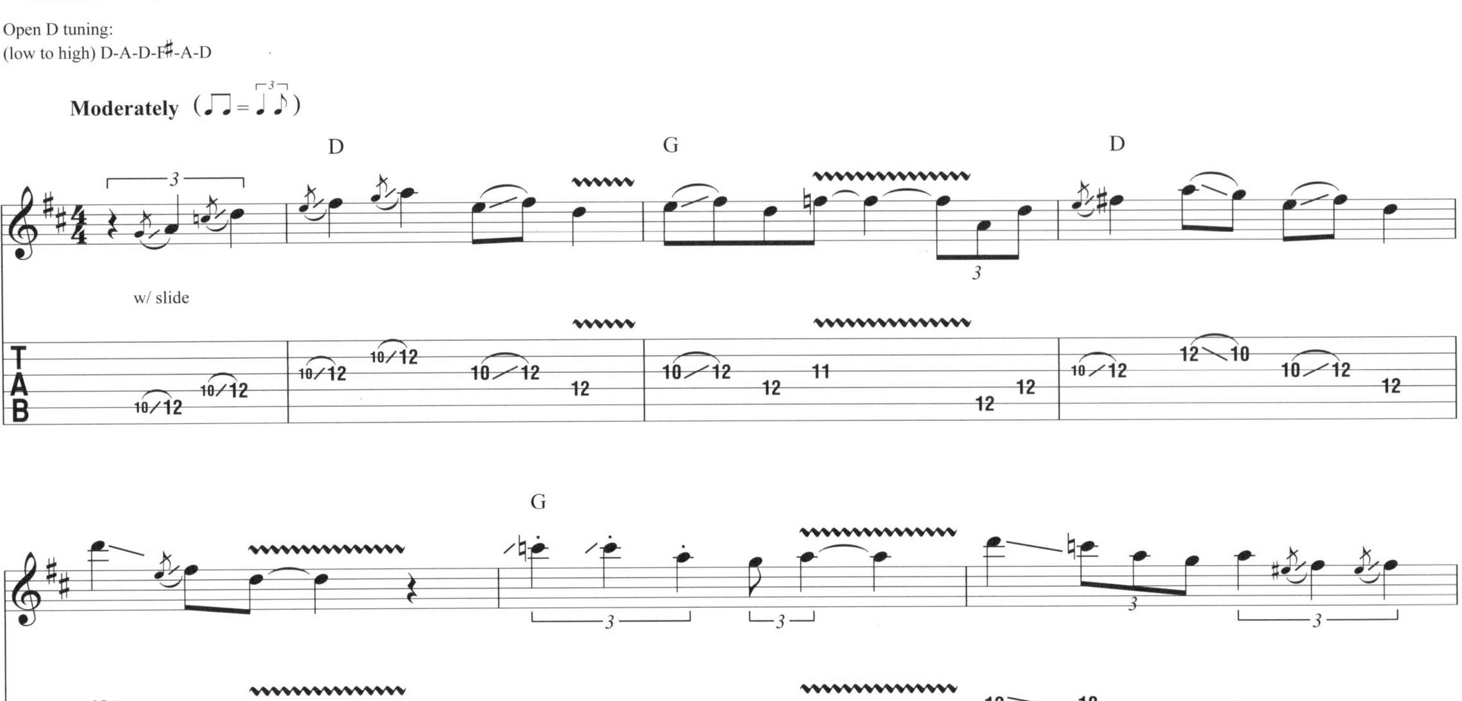

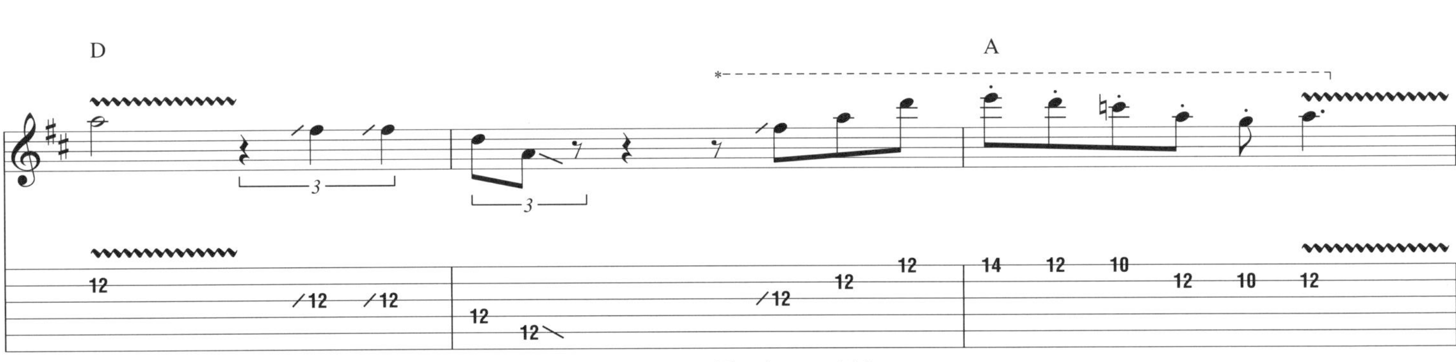

*Played as even eighth notes.

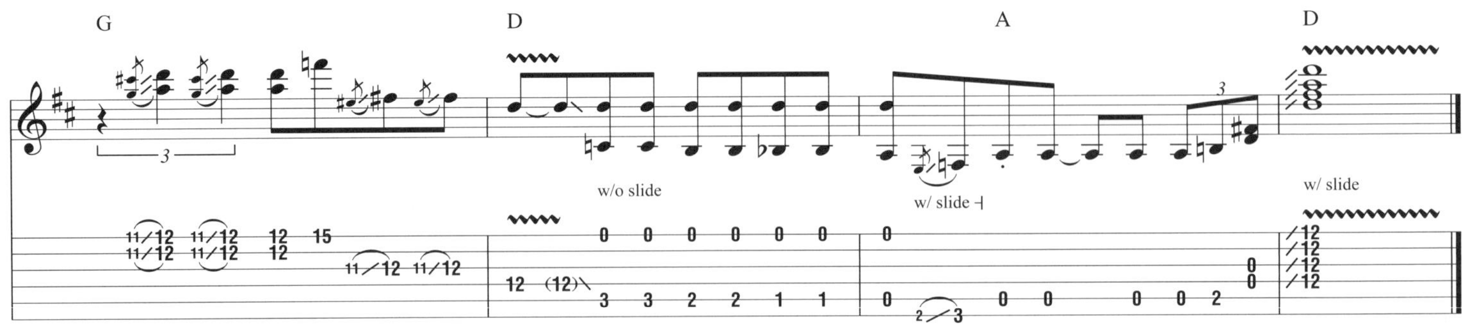

Fig. 48: And here is the turnaround from **Fig. 47** slowed down so it's easier to hear. It sounds good at a slower tempo, too. This turnaround has more harmonic content than the simpler walk-down and features lines played on string 3 (F♯).

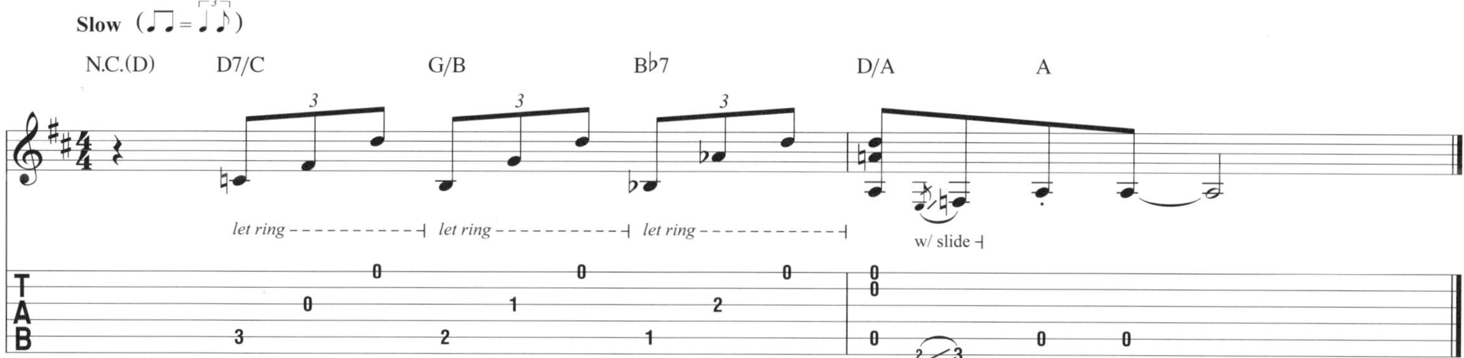

Blues Archaeology **In classical music theory, the effect of notes moving in the opposite direction simultaneously is known as "contrary motion." A famous example in rock music are the first chords in the verse of "Stairway to Heaven."**

Fig. 49: Here is the same open D turnaround as **Fig. 48**, slowed down with an ending added. It too sounds fine as a slow blues.

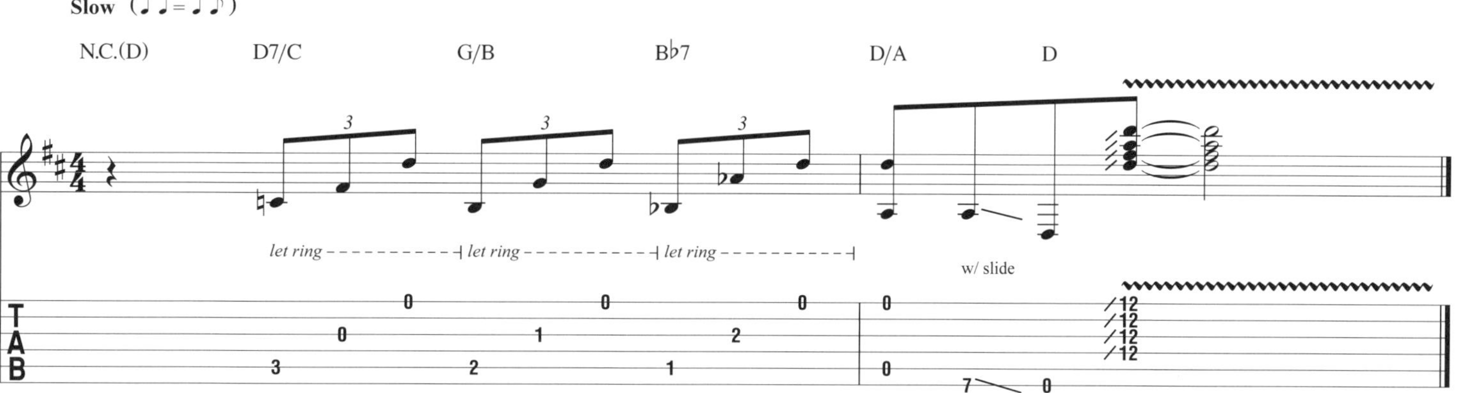

Fig. 50: Here I use Chicago blues slide guitar in standard tuning, key of C, as a voice over non-Chicago blues changes played on a second guitar. Except for one second of double-stop on the two high strings at the beginning of the bridge, I use single-note melodies like a voice or sax. After I recorded it, I noticed I gripped and used my thumb pick like a flat pick. Also, I picked with all down strokes, as many flat pickers do for clarity and assertiveness. That's what worked for me here to hit those notes as I felt them. I love to play slide guitar inspired by human and canine singing, and I often do it in standard tuning, where I'm already familiar with the locations of the notes. This non-standard chord progression aims for singing slide guitar that features Chicago blues, but also has a few sacred steel techniques, such as sliding into notes with sustain without picking them. This technique is carried on today by famous guitarists in the rock, blues, Americana, and soul styles. Here is one non-standard verse, bridge, and resolution.

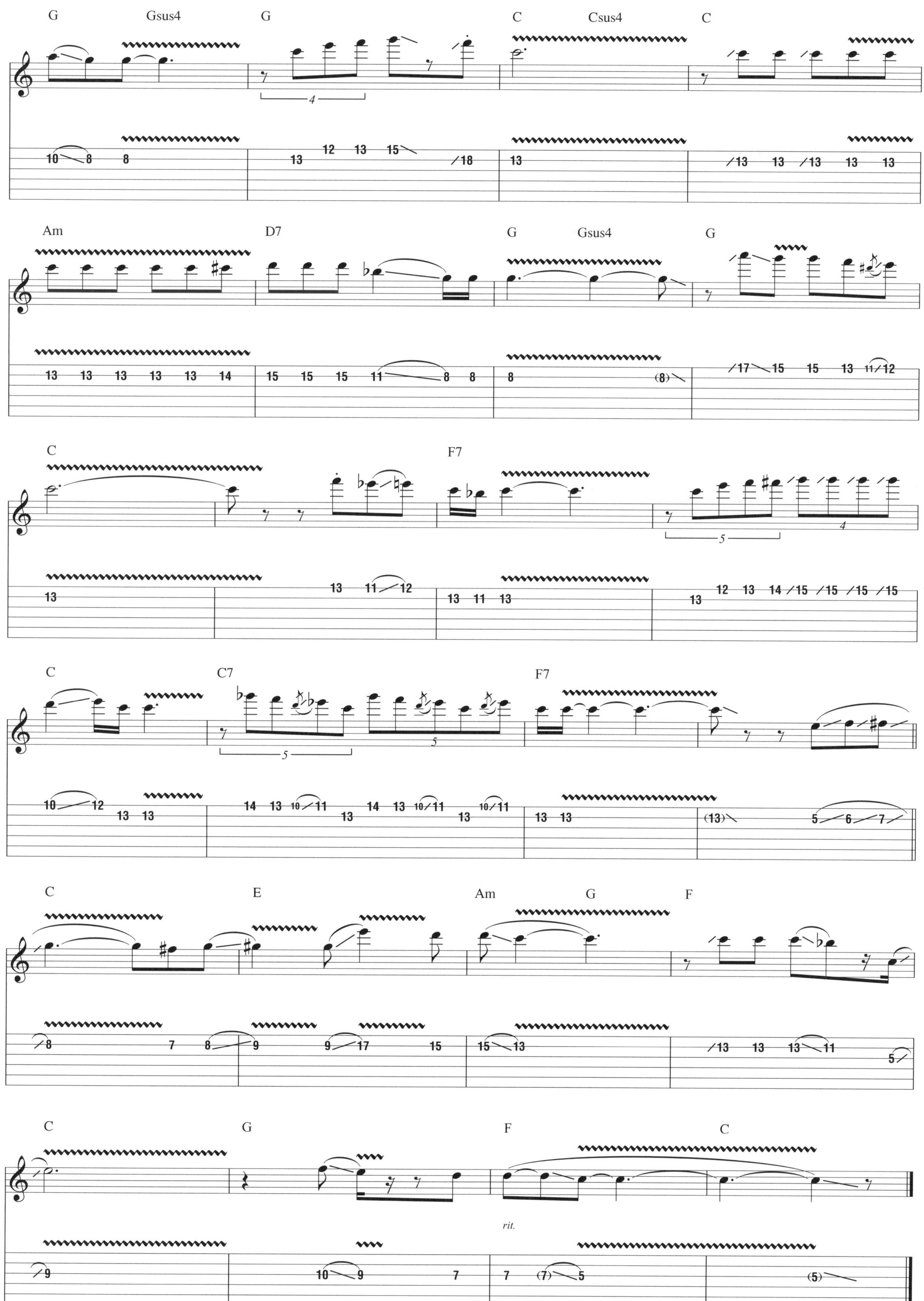
G
Gsus4
G
C
Csus4
C
Am
D7
G
Gsus4
G
C
F7
C
C7
F7
C
E
Am
G
F
C
G
F
C
rit.

Fig. 51: Here is open A minor solo blues guitar. I originally conceived the song in open G minor (as Muddy had done for a song we discussed earlier in the book), but when I recorded it, I tried and liked tuning one step up to open A minor for the clarity a higher register brings to guitar and vocal, if sung. While a lower key usually sounds sadder, the higher key for the guitar sounds (I hope) more urgently desperate.

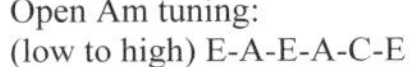

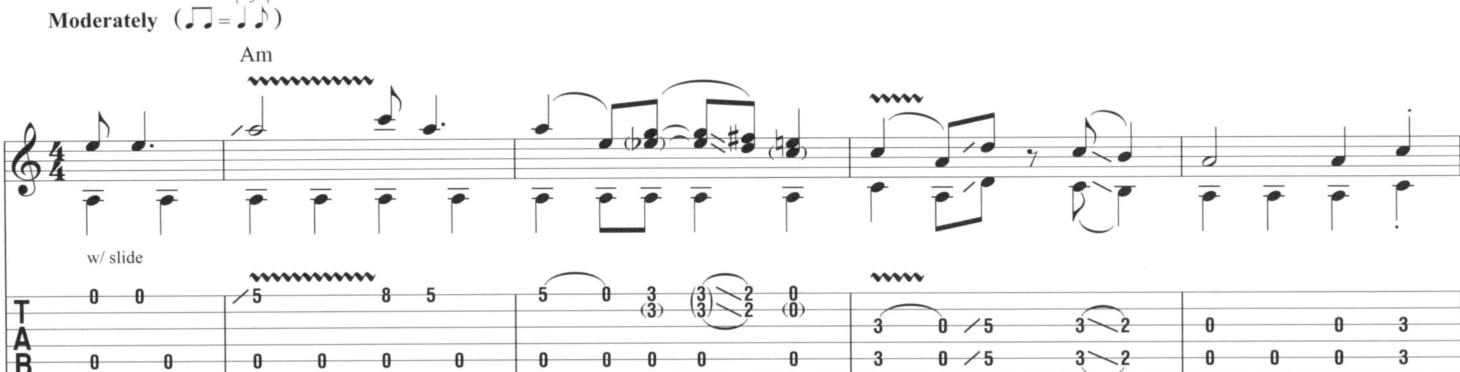

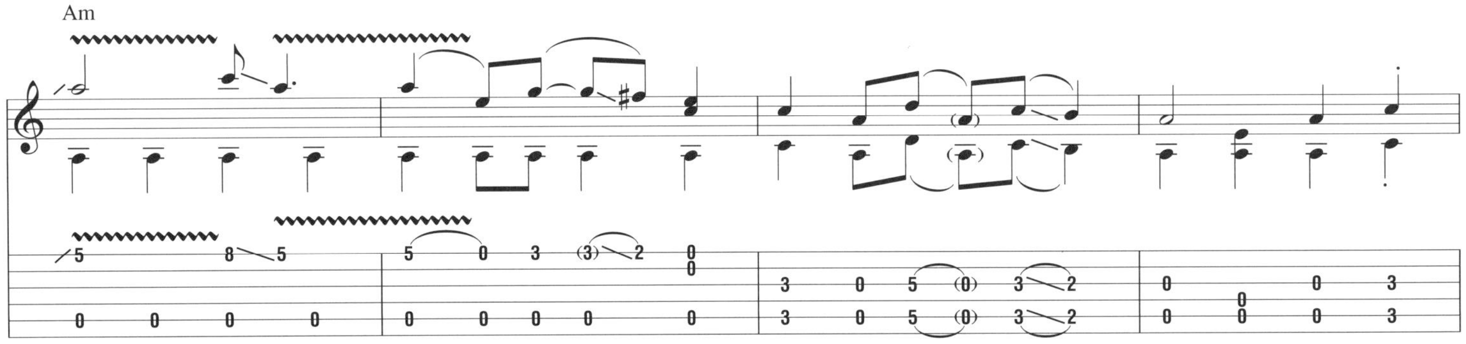

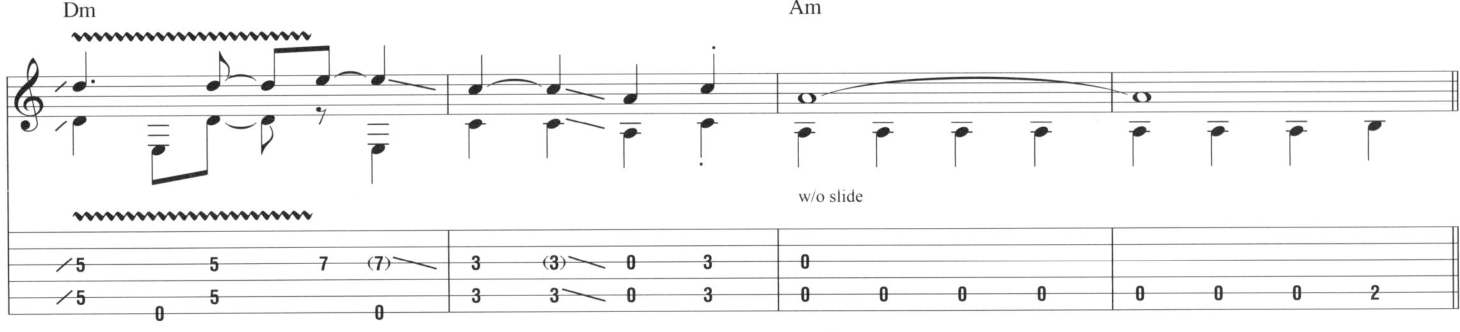

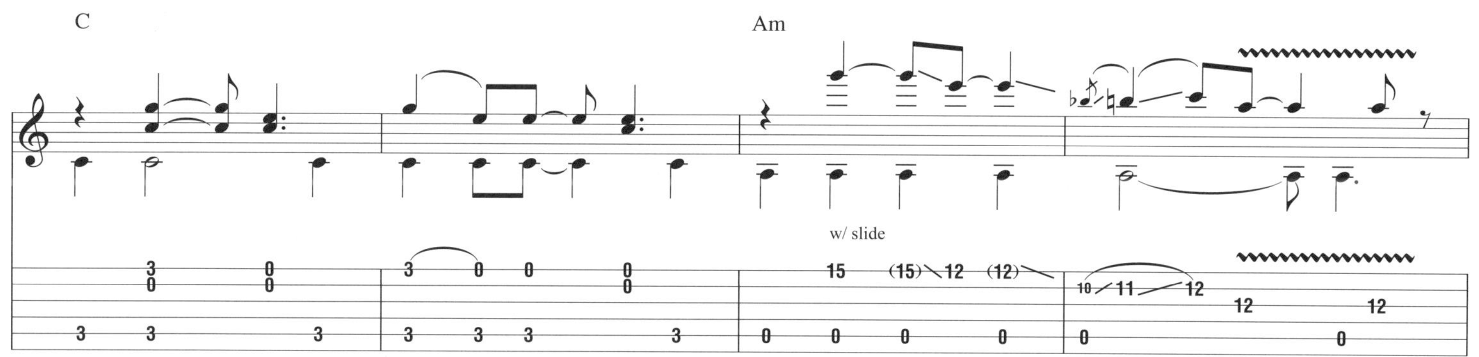

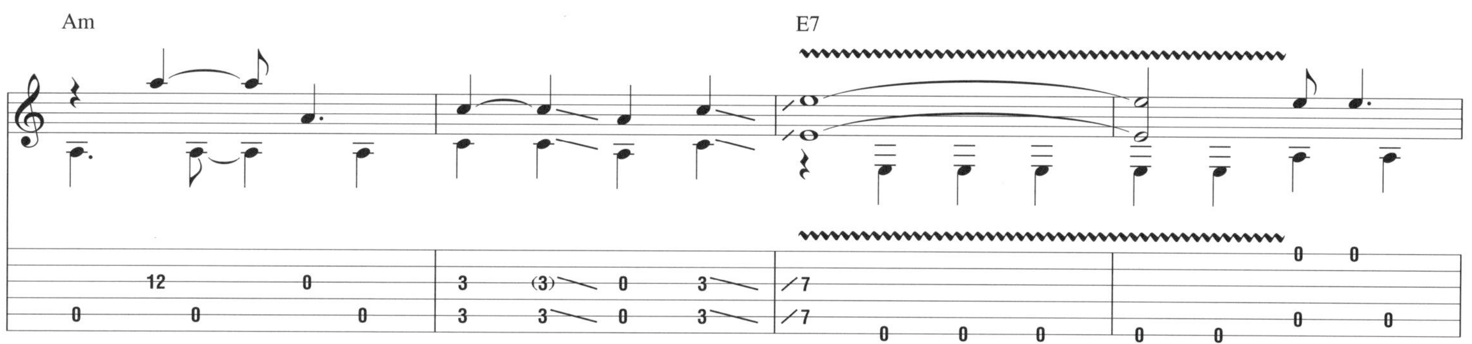

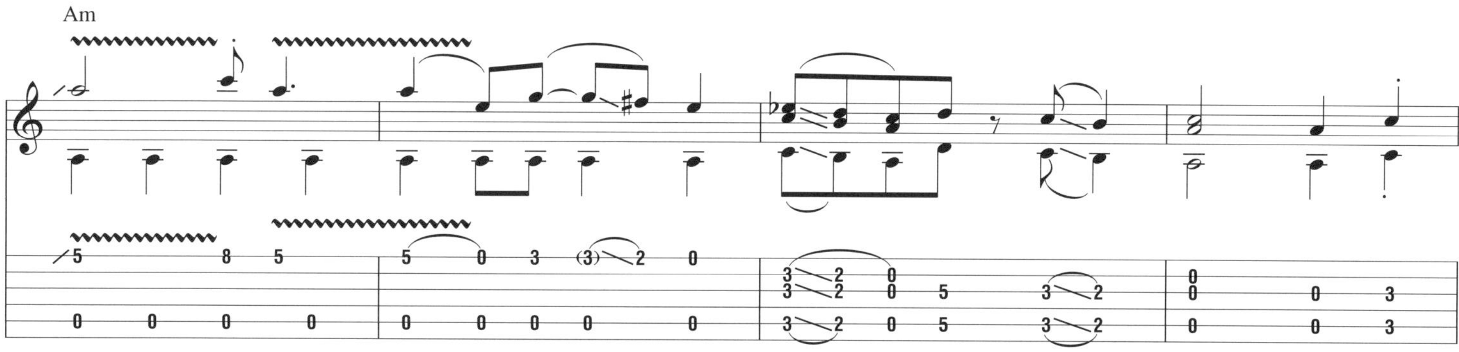

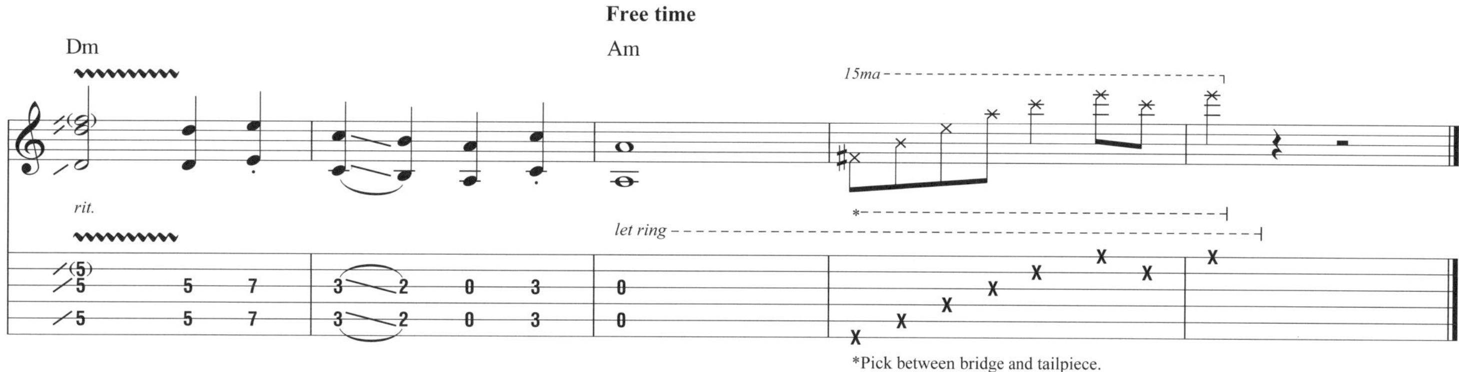

*Pick between bridge and tailpiece.

Fig. 52: One verse in the key of E with two guitars. Here is a slide melody "sung" in open E tuning as Chicago blues slide guitar over a non-Chicago progression. I used open E so I could let an open string ring as part of the melody. There is one rhythm guitar part and one "singing" slide guitar part.

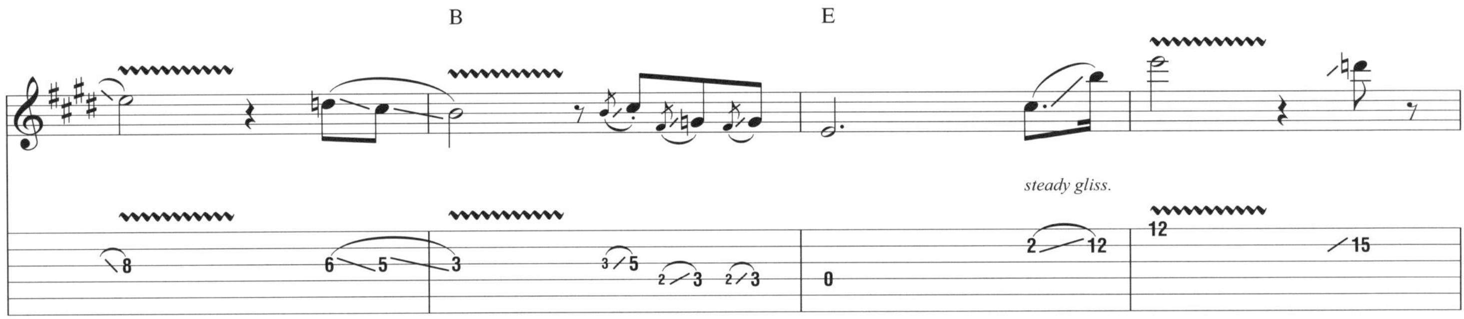

Blues Archaeology Although a recognized master of Chicago blues, Bob has musical interests and abilities beyond the standard forms and riffs of the genre. Nonetheless, because the spirit of the blues resides in his soul and fingers, his music always exudes it.

Fig. 53: Here, a background guitar plays a catchy hook riff on each chord change of blues chords in the key of E minor. The slide guitar is tuned to open E minor.

Open Em tuning:
(low to high) E-B-E-G-B-E

Moderately

Bm Am Em

w/ slide

Em

Am

Bm Em

Fig. 54: Medium tempo blues in G with a capo on fret 3. Thumping thumb drives the rhythm under the melody or solo.

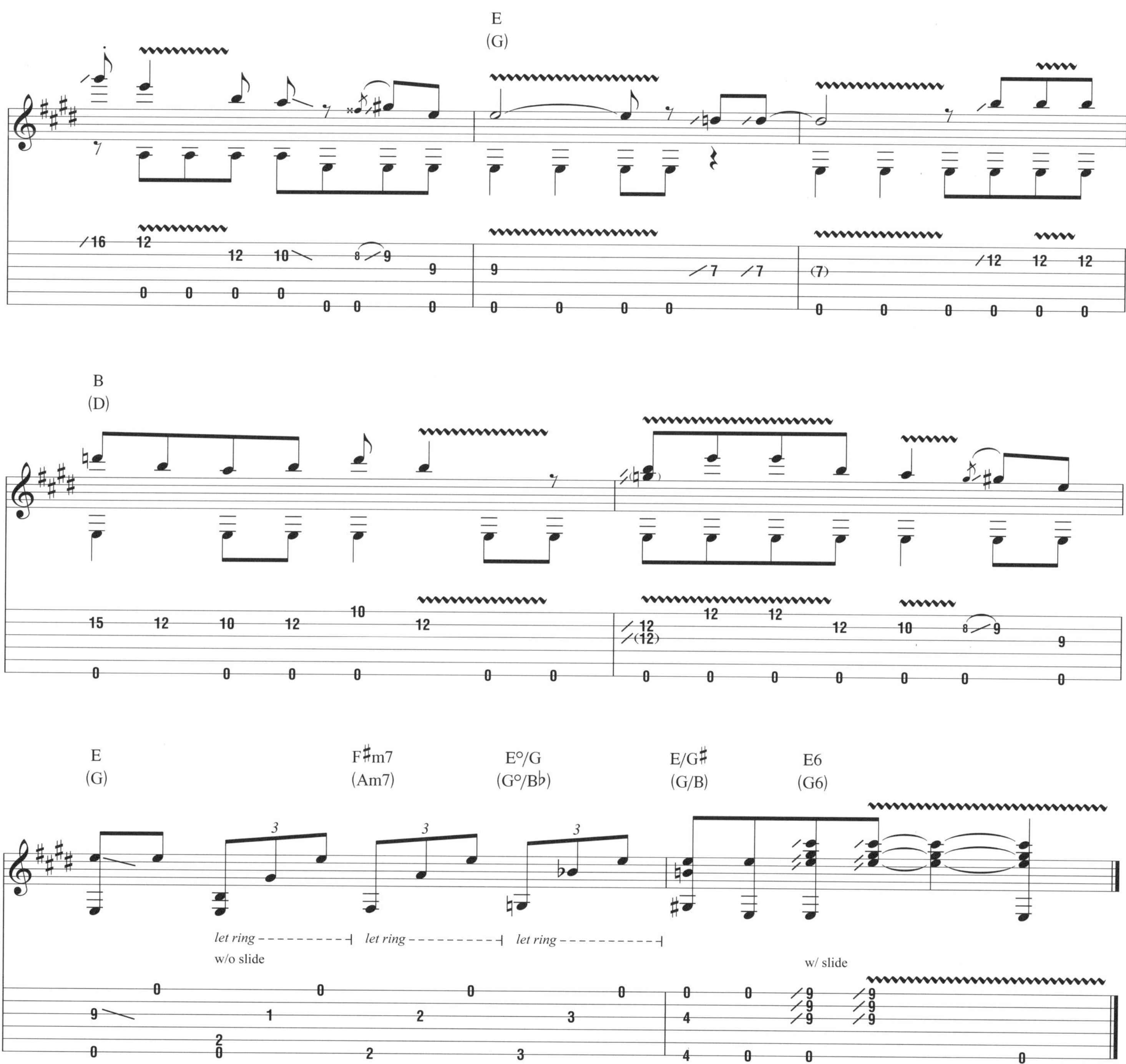

E
(G)
B
(D)
E
(G)
F♯m7
(Am7)
E°/G
(G°/B♭)
E/G♯
(G/B)
E6
(G6)
let ring
let ring
let ring
w/o slide
w/ slide

Fig. 55: Here is one guitar in open G in an 8-bar blues. The style "I ride" is classic Chicago blues slide guitar.

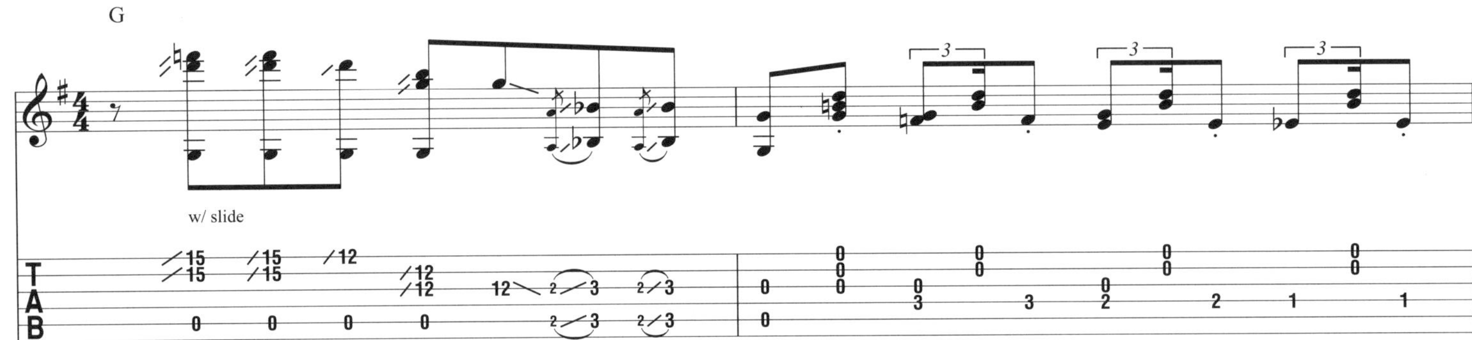

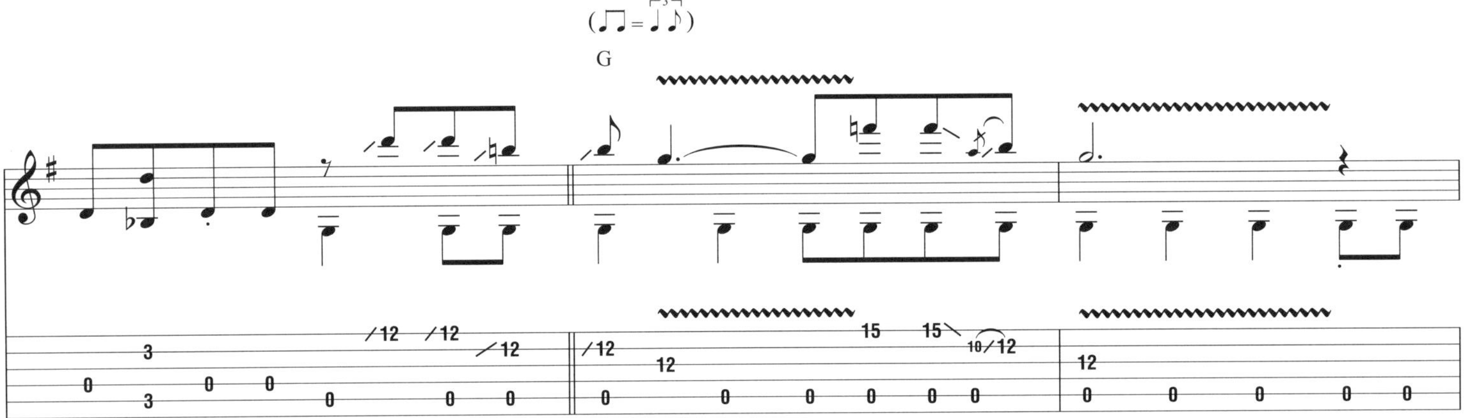

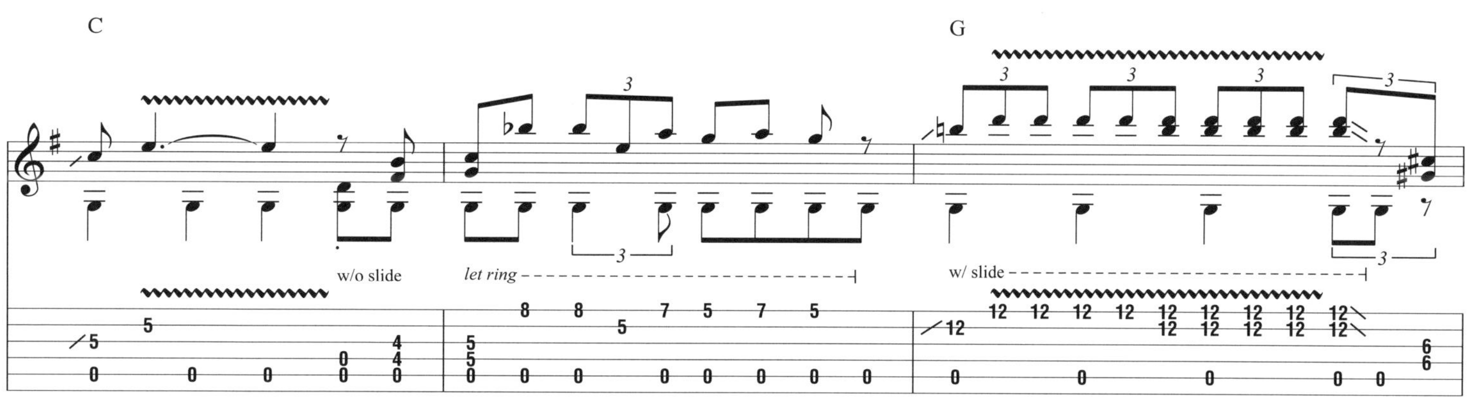

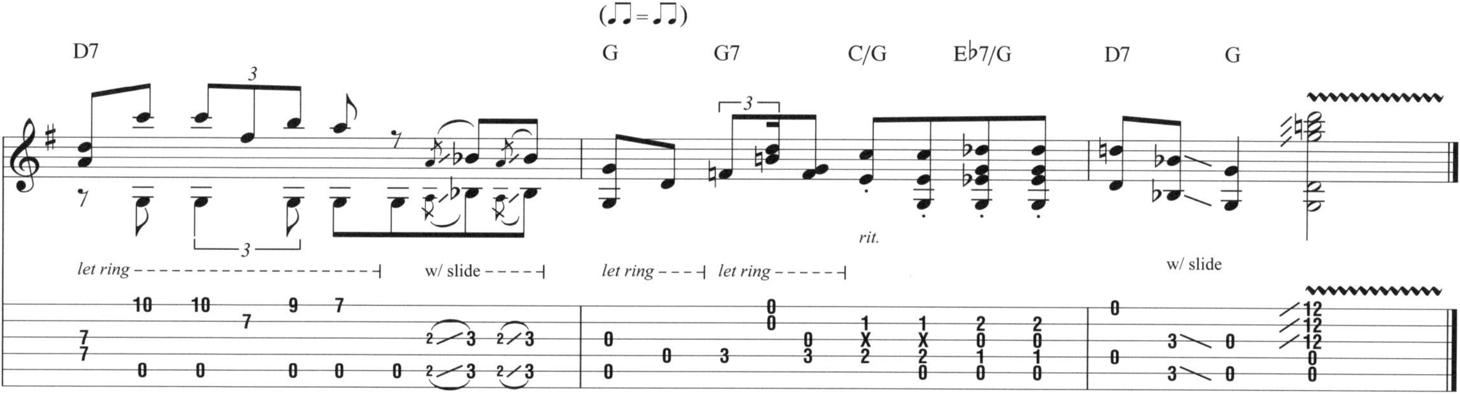

Blues Archaeology Muddy was influenced by Robert Johnson and Bob is influenced by Muddy. The lineage is here for all to hear and enjoy.

Fig. 56: This is a fast, Chicago-style, two-beat shuffle. The background guitar is in standard tuning and the slide is in open E.

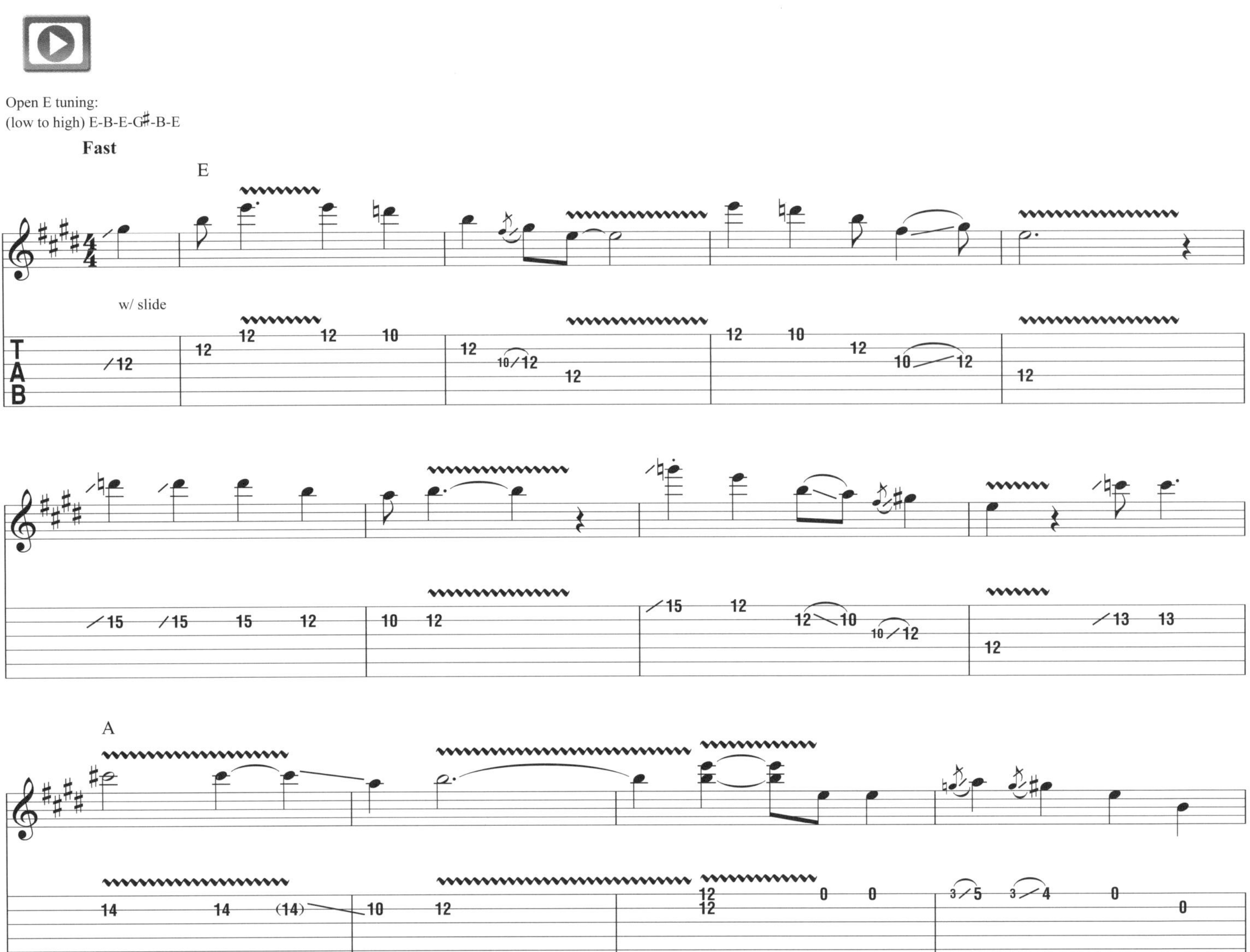

Blues Archaeology Bob's expertly executed slide has so much presence that when combined with a memorable melody, a stand-alone instrumental is created.

Fig. 57: Here's an instrumental using Chicago blues slide guitar to "sing" over Motown-style chord changes in the key of C. Rhythm guitar plays the changes while the slide guitar in open D tuning plays the vocal part.

Open D tuning:
(low to high) D-A-D-F♯-A-D

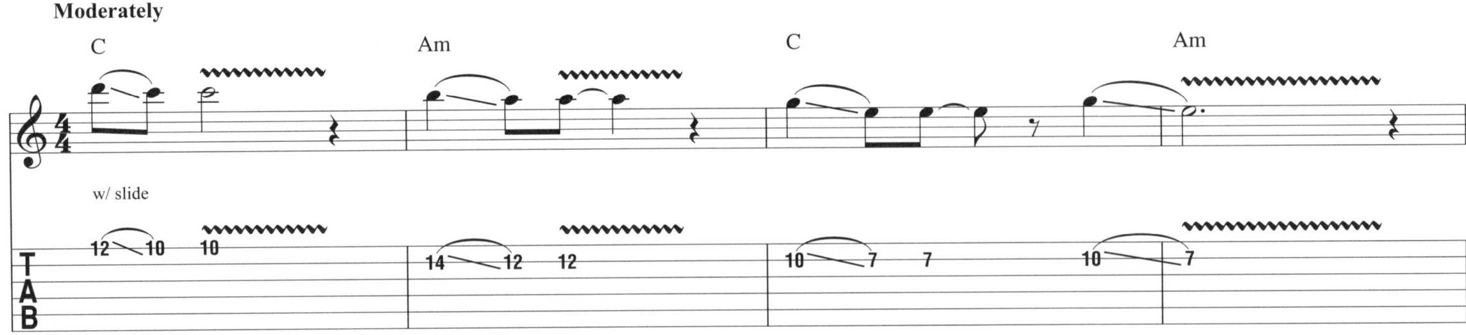

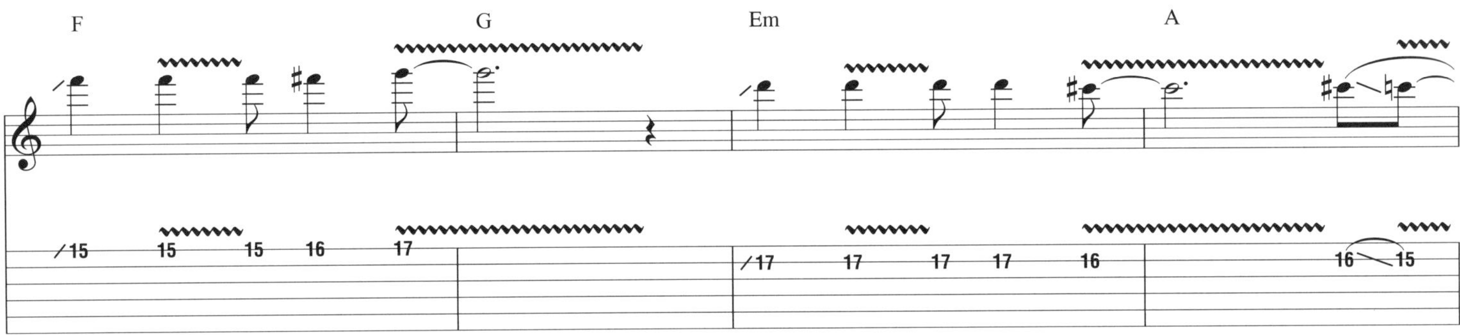

Blues Archaeology Bob has such nuanced control, he can make his slide notes sustain with legato phrasing to match a violin.

Fig. 58: Here's a verse of slow blues in open E minor tuning, using both slide and fretted notes.

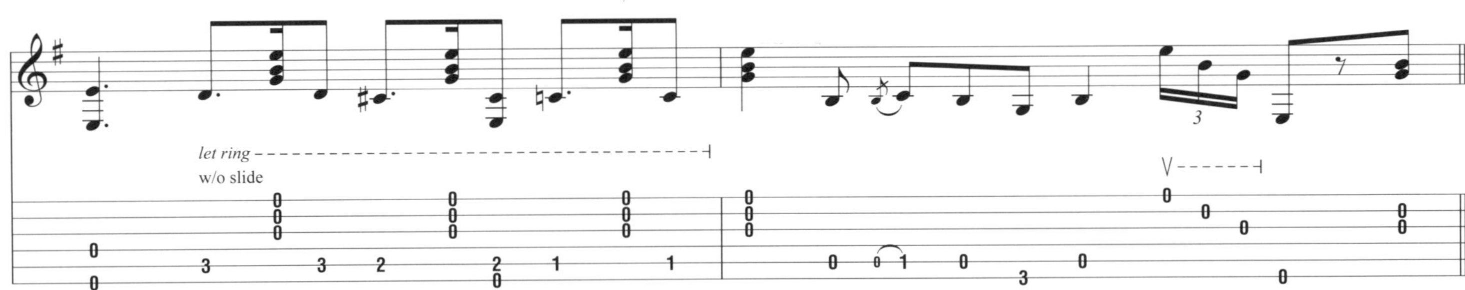

Blues Archaeology **Proving minor key blues can be elegiac as well as somber, Bob closes the book and his Master Class with a master performance.**

Stepping back for perspective at the end of this virtual workshop, my slide guitar style is a development of styles that influenced me, combined with decades of experience onstage and recording both original songs and covers. I use both the practice of open tunings (altered in the service of the song) and standard tuning (where the notes are familiar to standard-tuning players), but we slide to the notes we want, use the special slide vibrato, and add conventional fingering with the other fingers that don't slide. Some of my developments were conceived slowly and deliberately while songwriting and recording and others came to me while improvising onstage. I hope they will be useful to you in your own playing.

VIDEO GEAR

For recording the 58 videos, I chose my B&G Private Build Step Sister. The pickups are called Kikbuckers. They are single-coil, yet noiseless. The tones are greasy to elegant, and there are acoustic-sounding resonances and microphonics within them. This guitar plays easier than any in my experience. I am using a guitar made in 2018 to display every style of Chicago blues slide guitar, and you can judge real-world tone and playability compared to provenance for yourself. The old Tele on the cover of this book looks more vintage. Either guitar would have been fine for these videos; I used the Tele for our Hal Leonard book *Chicago Blues Rhythm Guitar*.

Blues Archaeology **The vintage guitars so many of us love were new and radical, especially the solid body ones, in the early 1950s. Someday, great contemporary guitars will be vintage, too.**

I play slide parts in the videos through a 1976 Music Man 2-10 Sixty-Five—two 10-inch speakers and 65 watts. I bought it right after borrowing Eric Clapton's Music Man amp to play with Muddy Waters at *The Last Waltz* in 1976. Onstage, it can play louder than a Super Reverb and almost as loud as a Twin Reverb. But it features a low-power switch and master volume control, so for these videos I had the capability to play with a Chicago blues, overdriven, "amp-about-to-explode" tone at low acoustic volume that balanced with my speaking voice. On some of the videos, I used reverb built into the amp and/or a Boss DD5 pedal for Chess Records-style slap echo.

I showed this amp to Johnny Winter as we began a 1977 tour for Muddy's *Hard Again* album. Johnny liked it so much he immediately got an endorsement from the company and used his Music Man amps for the rest of his life. I used this amp onstage from 1976 until about 1995. Muddy used this amp for his guitar on his 1978 *I'm Ready* album. Some of the supporting guitar parts in the videos for this book were pre-recorded on a computer and amplified through the second channel of the Music Man, but most were sent through an early 1950s Gibson GA-5 amp. For what it's worth, I retired my Music Man amp as soon as Victoria Amps started in 1994. All of their amps have great tone, but I don't own a Victoria that plays with distortion at a low enough volume for these videos.

I use large Golden Gate plastic thumb picks. The slide is chrome-plated metal, bought recently in a music store. The guitar strings are close to the gauge that Muddy Waters had me buy for him in the 1970s, which were Gibson Medium-Gauge with a .022 plain replacing the wound G string. I have found similar tone in GHS Super Steels, low to high: .056-.044-.032-.020(plain)-.016-.012. They are harder to bend than smaller strings, but they have a full tone, can take harder picking, and stay in tune better than lighter strings. I got used to bending or using finger vibrato with them; it takes more strength, but it's worth the effort. I keep the action at a height that accommodates both slide and fretted guitar styles.

STEADY ROLLIN' BOB MARGOLIN BIOGRAPHY

Bob Margolin is a world-renowned blues guitarist and singer. He played guitar in Muddy Waters' band from 1973–1980 and tours worldwide today as a bandleader or guest with both legendary and contemporary musicians. In the late 1970s, he played authentic Chicago blues guitar with Muddy on albums and in concerts and appeared with him at the original *Last Waltz* in 1976. He also recorded with Muddy and Johnny Winter in the late 1970s. Bob is a founding partner in the VizzTone Label Group, on the Board of Directors of the Pinetop Perkins Foundation, and is the Music Director of their Masterclass Workshops.

Many times between 2002–2018, Bob led workshops on "Raw Chicago Blues" at Jorma Kaukonen's Fur Peace Ranch, a "Magic Kingdom" for guitar workshops and concerts. He won Blues Music Awards for Guitar in 2005 and 2008, after being nominated in 1996. In 2017, he won Blues Blast Magazine Awards for "Best Male Blues Artist" and "Traditional Album of the Year," and a Blues Music Award for "Best Traditional Blues Male Artist."

In 2011, his eBook *Steady Rollin'* was published, and he received the 2013 "Keeping the Blues Alive Award in Journalism" in appreciation of his 20 years writing for *Blues Revue*. His 2016 album *My Road* received chart-topping blues radio airplay and critical acclaim. It revealed Bob's musical history and what he is doing today, a sonic demonstration of both Chicago blues rhythm guitar and Chicago blues slide guitar. In addition, beginning in 2016 and through March 2020, he toured the world as a guest or bandleader.

Bob was featured in *The Last Waltz 2019 All-Star Tour* with Warren Haynes, Jamey Johnson, Lukas Nelson, Taj Mahal, John Medeski, Danny Louis, and Michael McDonald. Bob played at the original *Last Waltz* with Muddy Waters, Paul Butterfield, and the Band. Some celebration shows included original *Last Waltz* partners Garth Hudson, Robbie Robertson, Emmylou Harris, and Dr. John. When Bob plays Muddy's song "Mannish Boy," he now adds Chicago blues slide guitar to the song, wishing he could go back in time and do it with Muddy and the Band. He reports, "Slide guitar gets the audience immediately from the first note of the introduction I play."

Bob's self-titled 2018 album was well-reviewed and took a step deeper, as he played and recorded every note on the album in a self-produced venture. In 2018–2019, Bob played shows with Jimmy Vivino called "Just 2 Guitars & 200 Stories" and toured the U.S. and Europe. In 2020, he played on an all-star *Tribute to B.B. King* and took the opportunity to play standard-tuning slide guitar when leading on one of B.B.'s songs. Likewise in 2020, Bob's all-acoustic album *This Guitar and Tonight* won the Blues Blast Magazine Award for "Best Acoustic Album," along with the "Blues Music Award" in the same category. Later in the year, his EP *Falling Star of Stage and Screens* was released as a musical take on the tragedy, outrage, loss of live music, and political issues of the "Covid Era." Please find current information on *www.bobmargolin.com* and Bob's Facebook pages.

ESSENTIAL CHICAGO BLUES SLIDE GUITAR RECORDINGS

Various Artists – *Bottles, Knives & Steel Vol. 1 and 2* (Columbia): This "Slide 101" course of 39 songs is the one to take for a comprehensive overview of everyone from Sylvester Weaver to lesser-known but equally worthy 'neckers like Casey Bill Weldon and Buddy Moss. Includes Weaver's "Guitar Rag," Blind Willie Johnson's "Dark Was the Night," and his "God Don't Never Change."

Tampa Red – *It's Tight Like That* (Story): Eighteen hokum and straight blues tunes from 1928–1942 that still have the ability to amaze and delight. His eloquent instrumental version of Leroy Carr's classic "How Long, How Long Blues" (the source of Robert Johnson's "Come On in My Kitchen") is worth the price of admission alone, as is "Bumble Bee Blues," where he conjures slide and fingered passages like a musical magician.

Elmore James – *Dust My Broom* (Tomato): The CD for when you just *have* to hear the "...Broom" riff on the epochal title tune and its variations "Baby Please Set a Date" and "Talk to Me." In addition, the 15 classics also feature James on the aching, broken-hearted slow blues "The Sky Is Crying" and "Something Inside Me," where the triplet king gets *almost* jazzy over the "Stormy Monday"-type chord substitutions.

Hound Dog Taylor – *Deluxe Edition* (Alligator): Low down, dirty, and nasty slide played loose and loud by the Houserockers for the sheer hell of it. Fifteen selections from Taylor's first three studio albums include rhythm/bass guitarist Brewer Phillips' outrageous "Phillips Goes Bananas." Let's boogie, baby!

Muddy Waters – *Best of Muddy Waters* (Chess) and ***Muddy "Mississippi" Waters Live Legacy Edition*** reissue (Friday Music): Just two of many essential Muddy albums featuring his soul-piercing, signature slide guitar.

GUITAR NOTATION LEGEND

Guitar music can be notated three different ways: on a *musical staff*, in *tablature*, and in *rhythm slashes*.

RHYTHM SLASHES are written above the staff. Strum chords in the rhythm indicated. Use the chord diagrams found at the top of the first page of the transcription for the appropriate chord voicings. Round noteheads indicate single notes.

THE MUSICAL STAFF shows pitches and rhythms and is divided by bar lines into measures. Pitches are named after the first seven letters of the alphabet.

TABLATURE graphically represents the guitar fingerboard. Each horizontal line represents a string, and each number represents a fret.

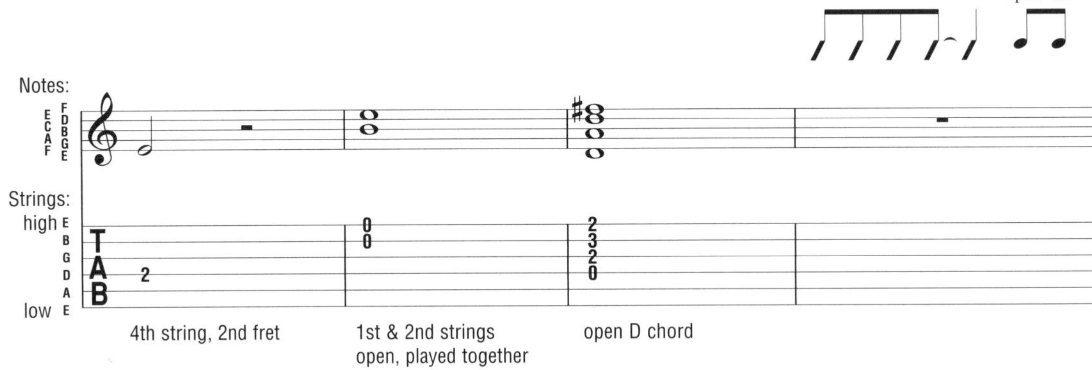

Definitions for Special Guitar Notation

HALF-STEP BEND: Strike the note and bend up 1/2 step.

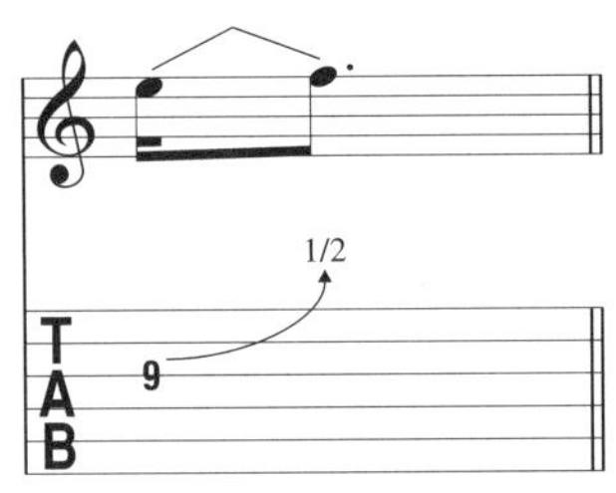

WHOLE-STEP BEND: Strike the note and bend up one step.

GRACE NOTE BEND: Strike the note and immediately bend up as indicated.

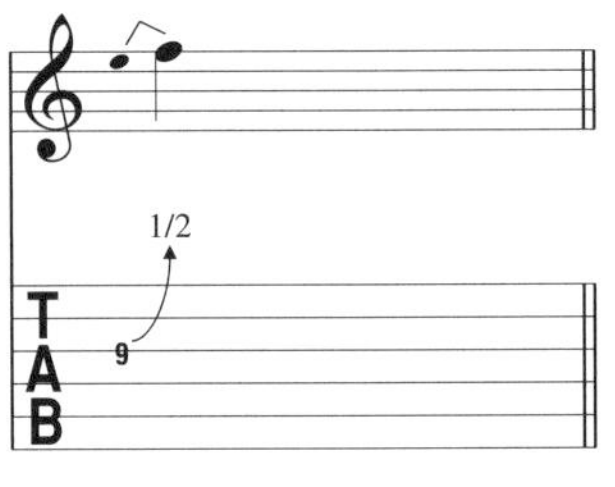

SLIGHT (MICROTONE) BEND: Strike the note and bend up 1/4 step.

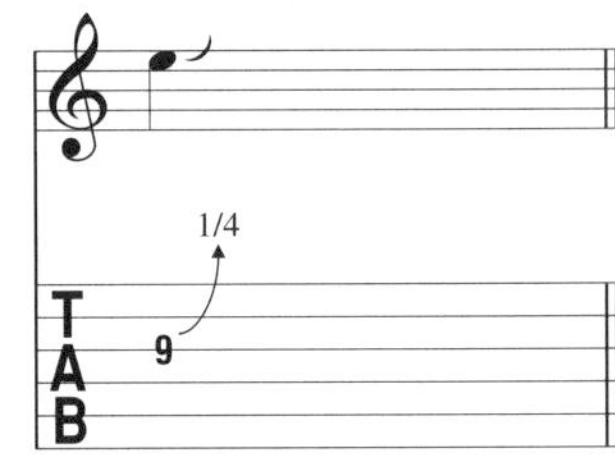

BEND AND RELEASE: Strike the note and bend up as indicated, then release back to the original note. Only the first note is struck.

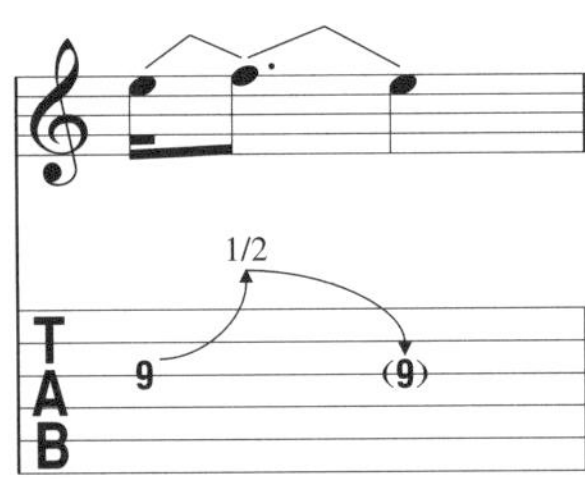

PRE-BEND: Bend the note as indicated, then strike it.

PRE-BEND AND RELEASE: Bend the note as indicated. Strike it and release the bend back to the original note.

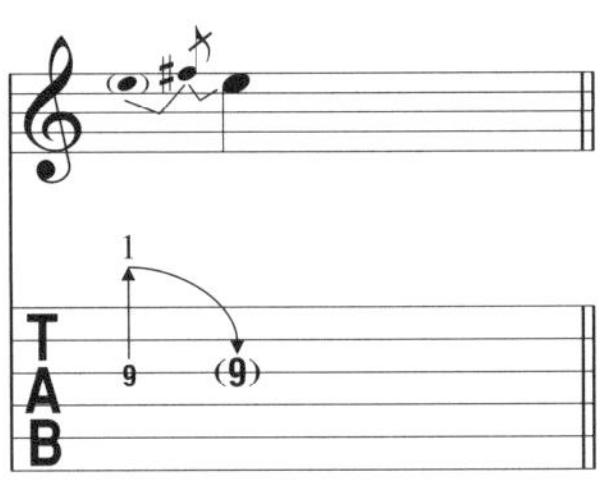

UNISON BEND: Strike the two notes simultaneously and bend the lower note up to the pitch of the higher.

VIBRATO: The string is vibrated by rapidly bending and releasing the note with the fretting hand.

WIDE VIBRATO: The pitch is varied to a greater degree by vibrating with the fretting hand.

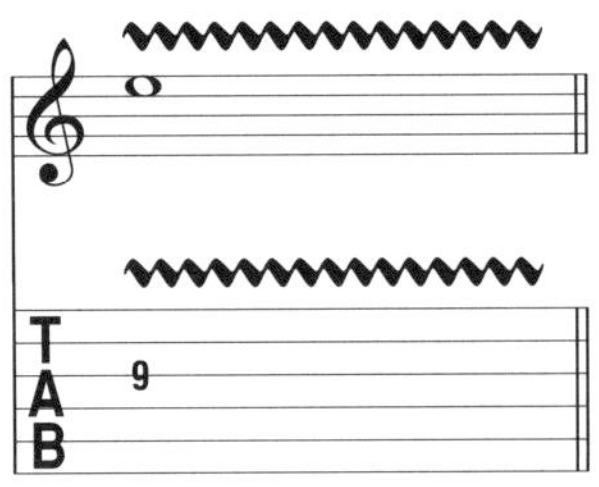

HAMMER-ON: Strike the first (lower) note with one finger, then sound the higher note (on the same string) with another finger by fretting it without picking.

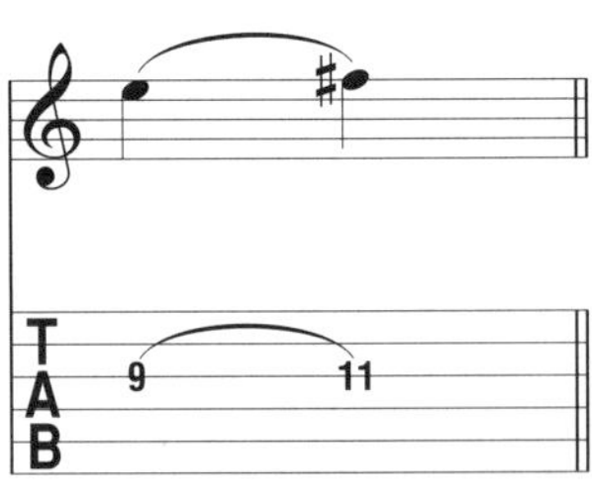

PULL-OFF: Place both fingers on the notes to be sounded. Strike the first note and without picking, pull the finger off to sound the second (lower) note.

LEGATO SLIDE: Strike the first note and then slide the same fret-hand finger up or down to the second note. The second note is not struck.

SHIFT SLIDE: Same as legato slide, except the second note is struck.

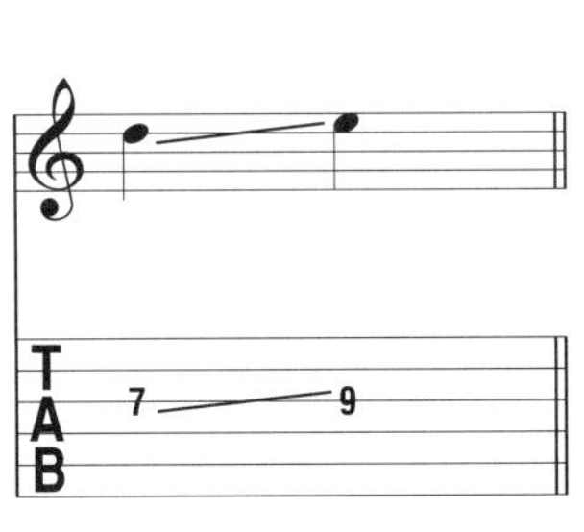

TRILL: Very rapidly alternate between the notes indicated by continuously hammering on and pulling off.

TAPPING: Hammer ("tap") the fret indicated with the pick-hand index or middle finger and pull off to the note fretted by the fret hand.

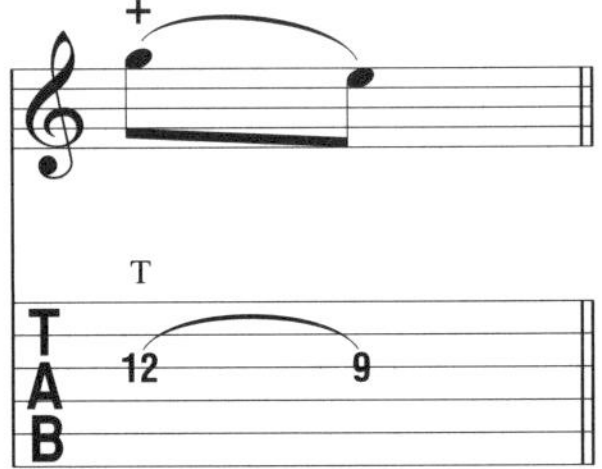

NATURAL HARMONIC: Strike the note while the fret-hand lightly touches the string directly over the fret indicated.

PINCH HARMONIC: The note is fretted normally and a harmonic is produced by adding the edge of the thumb or the tip of the index finger of the pick hand to the normal pick attack.

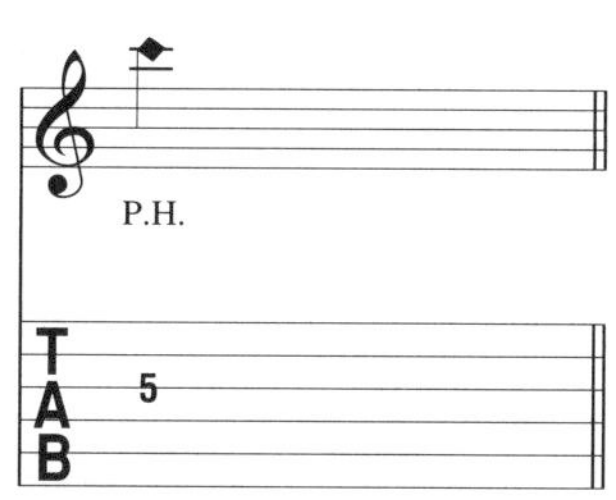

HARP HARMONIC: The note is fretted normally and a harmonic is produced by gently resting the pick hand's index finger directly above the indicated fret (in parentheses) while the pick hand's thumb or pick assists by plucking the appropriate string.

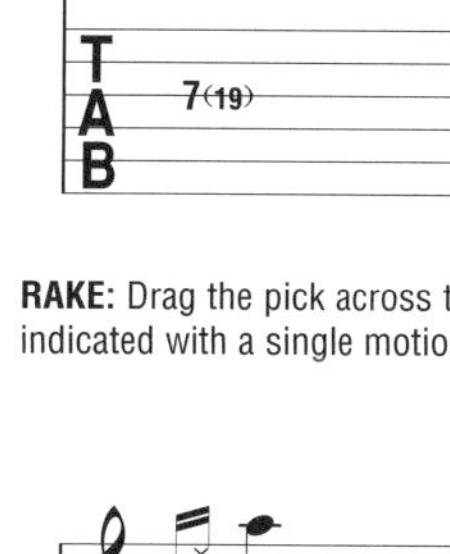

PICK SCRAPE: The edge of the pick is rubbed down (or up) the string, producing a scratchy sound.

MUFFLED STRINGS: A percussive sound is produced by laying the fret hand across the string(s) without depressing, and striking them with the pick hand.

PALM MUTING: The note is partially muted by the pick hand lightly touching the string(s) just before the bridge.

RAKE: Drag the pick across the strings indicated with a single motion.

TREMOLO PICKING: The note is picked as rapidly and continuously as possible.

ARPEGGIATE: Play the notes of the chord indicated by quickly rolling them from bottom to top.

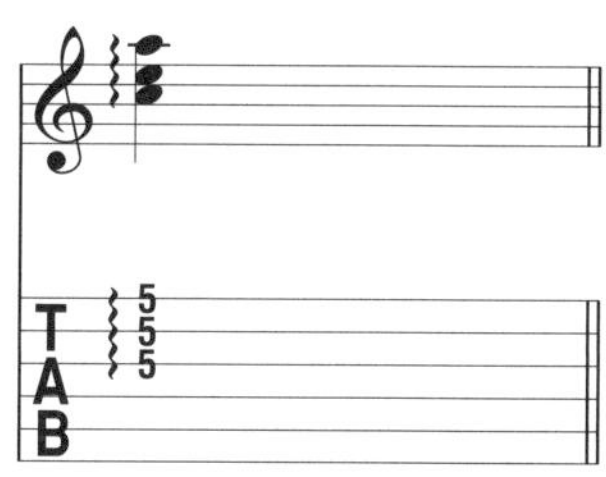

VIBRATO BAR DIVE AND RETURN: The pitch of the note or chord is dropped a specified number of steps (in rhythm), then returned to the original pitch.

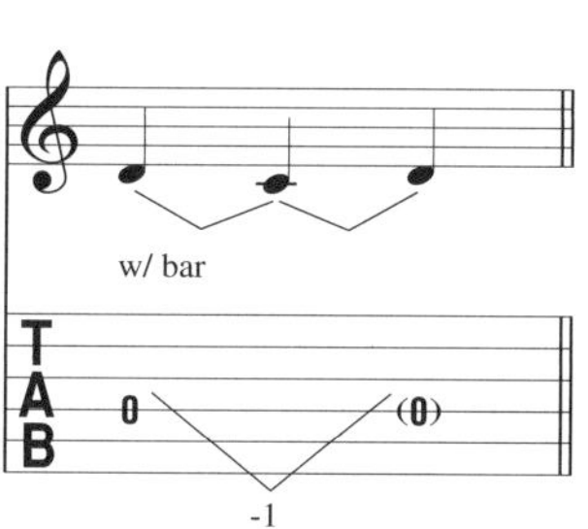

VIBRATO BAR SCOOP: Depress the bar just before striking the note, then quickly release the bar.

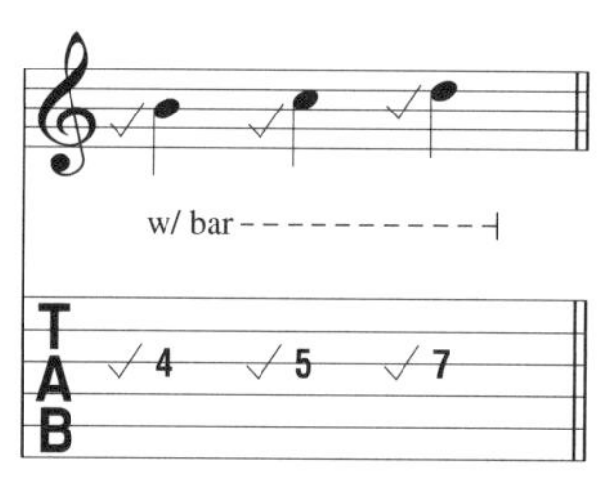

VIBRATO BAR DIP: Strike the note and then immediately drop a specified number of steps, then release back to the original pitch.

Additional Musical Definitions

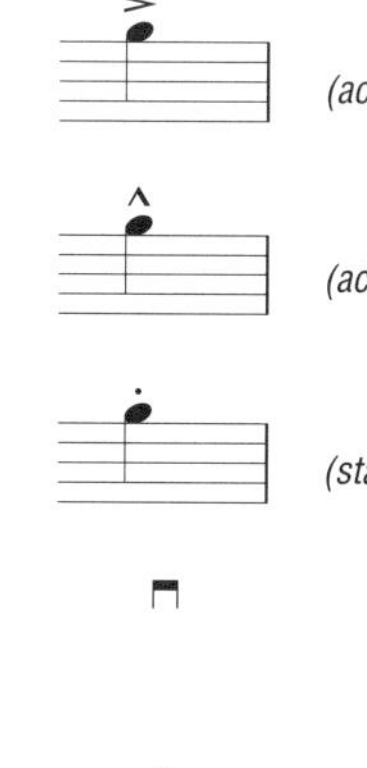

(accent) • Accentuate note (play it louder).

(accent) • Accentuate note with great intensity.

(staccato) • Play the note short.

• Downstroke

V • Upstroke

D.S. al Coda • Go back to the sign (𝄋), then play until the measure marked "***To Coda***," then skip to the section labelled "**Coda.**"

D.C. al Fine • Go back to the beginning of the song and play until the measure marked "***Fine***" (end).

Rhy. Fig. • Label used to recall a recurring accompaniment pattern (usually chordal).

Riff • Label used to recall composed, melodic lines (usually single notes) which recur.

Fill • Label used to identify a brief melodic figure which is to be inserted into the arrangement.

Rhy. Fill • A chordal version of a Fill.

tacet • Instrument is silent (drops out).

• Repeat measures between signs.

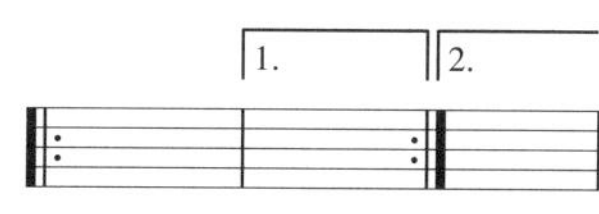

• When a repeated section has different endings, play the first ending only the first time and the second ending only the second time.

NOTE: Tablature numbers in parentheses mean:

1. The note is being sustained over a system (note in standard notation is tied), or
2. The note is sustained, but a new articulation (such as a hammer-on, pull-off, slide or vibrato) begins, or
3. The note is a barely audible "ghost" note (note in standard notation is also in parentheses).

MASTER THE *Blues*

BLUES GUITAR Instruction Books from Hal Leonard

All books include notes & tablature

12-Bar Blues
by Dave Rubin

The term "12-bar blues" has become synonymous with blues music and is the basis for other forms of popular music. This book is devoted to providing guitarists with all the technical tools necessary for playing 12-bar blues with authority. Covers: boogie, shuffle, swing, riff, and jazzy blues progressions; Chicago, minor, slow, bebop, and other blues styles; soloing, intros, turnarounds, and more.
00695187 Book/Online Audio..............$18.99

75 Blues Turnarounds
by Michael DoCampo with Toby Wine

This book/audio pack teaches 75 turnarounds over common chord progressions in a variety of styles, including those of blues guitar greats like Albert King, Johnny Winter, Mike Bloomfield, Duane Allman, Jeff Beck, T-Bone Walker and others.
02501043 Book/Online Audio..............$12.99

100 Blues Lessons
Guitar Lesson Goldmine
by John Heussenstamm and Chad Johnson

A huge variety of blues guitar styles and techniques are covered, including: turnarounds, hammer-ons and pull-offs, slides, the blues scale, 12-bar blues, double stops, muting techniques, hybrid picking, fingerstyle blues, and much more!
00696452 Book/Online Audio..............$24.99

101 Must-Know Blues Licks
by Wolf Marshall

Now you can add authentic blues feel and flavor to your playing! Here are 101 definitive licks – plus a demonstration CD – from every major blues guitar style, neatly organized into easy-to-use categories. They're all here, including Delta blues, jump blues, country blues, Memphis blues, Texas blues, West Coast blues, Chicago blues, and British blues.
00695318 Book/Online Audio..............$17.99

Beginning Blues Guitar
by Dave Rubin

From B.B. King and Buddy Guy to Eric Clapton and Stevie Ray Vaughan, blues guitar is a constant in American popular music. This book teaches the concepts and techniques fostered by legendary blues guitar players: 12-bar blues; major & minor pentatonic scales; the blues scale; string bending; licks; double-stops; intros and turnarounds; and more.
00695916 Book/Online Audio..............$12.99

Beginning Fingerstyle Blues Guitar
by Arnie Berle & Mark Galbo

A step-by-step method for learning this rich and powerful style. Takes you from the fundamentals of fingerpicking to five authentic blues tunes. Includes graded exercises, illustrated tips, plus standard notation and tablature.
14003799 Book/CD Pack....................$21.95

Brave New Blues Guitar
by Greg Koch

A kaleidoscopic reinterpretation of 16 blues rock titans is the hallmark of this Greg Koch book with over three hours of online video lessons. It breaks down the styles, techniques, and licks of guitarists including Albert Collins, B.B. King, Eric Clapton, Jimi Hendrix, Stevie Ray Vaughan, Johnny Winter and more.
00201987 Book/Online Video.............$19.99

Chicago Blues Rhythm Guitar
by Bob Margolin & Dave Rubin

This definitive instructional guitar book features loads of rhythm guitar playing examples to learn and practice, covering a variety of styles, techniques, tips, historical anecdotes, and much more. To top it off, every playing example in the book is performed on the accompanying DVD by Bob Margolin himself!
00121575 Book/DVD Pack.................$19.99

Everything About Playing the Blues
by Wilbur Savidge

An ideal reference guide to playing the blues for all guitarists. Full instruction on blues theory, chords, rhythm, scales, advanced solo technique, beginnings and endings, riff construction and more. Includes play-along audio with 12 jam tracks.
14010625 Book/Online Audio...............$29.99

Fretboard Roadmaps – Blues Guitar
by Fred Sokolow

Fretboard patterns are roadmaps that all great blues guitarists know and use. This book teaches how to: play lead and rhythm anywhere on the fretboard; play a variety of lead guitar styles; play chords and progressions anywhere on the fretboard, in any key; expand chord vocabulary; learn to think musically, the way the pros do.
00695350 Book/Online Audio..............$15.99

Hal Leonard Blues Guitar Method
by Greg Koch

Real blues songs are used to teach the basics of rhythm and lead blues guitar in the style of B.B. King, Buddy Guy, Eric Clapton, and many others. Lessons include: 12-bar blues; chords, scales and licks; vibrato and string bending; riffs, turnarounds, and boogie patterns; and more!
00697326 Book/Online Audio..............$16.99

How to Play Blues-Fusion Guitar
by Joe Charupakorn

Study the scales, chords, and arpeggios most commonly used in the blues-fusion style and how to use them in this book. You'll also examine how artists like Matt Schofield, Mike Stern, Scott Henderson, and John Scofield put their own spin on the blues/fusion format.
00137813 Book/Online Audio..............$19.99

Blues You Can Use Series
by John Ganapes

Blues You Can Use
This comprehensive source for learning blues guitar is designed to develop both your lead and rhythm playing. Blues styles covered include Texas, Delta, R&B, early rock & roll, gospel and blues/rock.
00142420 Book/Online Media..........................$19.99

More Blues You Can Use
This follow up edition covers: pentatonic scales, single-note tremolo, double-string bends, reverse bends, shuffle rhythms, 6th and 9th chords, boogie patterns, chord substitutions, vibrato techniques, and more!
00695165 Book/Online Audio........................$19.99

Blues Guitar Chords You Can Use
A reference guide to blues, R&B, jazz, and rock rhythm guitar, with hundreds of voicings, chord theory construction, chord progressions and exercises and much more.
00695082..$17.99

Blues Licks You Can Use
Contains music and performance notes for 75 hot lead phrases, covering styles including up-tempo and slow blues, jazz-blues, shuffle blues, swing blues and more!
00695386 Book/Online Audio..........................$16.99

Blues Rhythms You Can Use
Develop your rhythm playing chops with 21 progressive lessons: basic rhythm theory; major and minor blues; 8th, 16th and triplets; extensions; passing chords; lead-rhythm style; funky blues; jump blues; blues rock; and more.
00696038 Book/Online Audio..........................$19.99

Order these and more publications from your favorite music retailer at **halleonard.com**

1020
312

Prices, availability, and contents subject to change without notice.